1001 FUN THINGS TO DO IN RETIREMENT

MIKE BELLAH, PH.D.

 PRESS
CANYON, TX

Published by BestYears Press, Canyon, Texas, USA.

Book cover design by Robert Henslin – www.rhdcreative.com

Interior design by Rich Bullock – www.perilousfiction.com

Artwork by Lee Baughman

P 4/6/22

To my good friend Shug
—who has brought laughter and fun to my retirement years.

Table of Contents

"The settled happiness and security we all desire God withholds from us by the very nature of the world; but joy, pleasure and merriment he has scattered broadcast. We are never safe, but we have plenty of fun."

— C.S. Lewis

Introduction

A Primer On Playfulness

Why write a book like this? Don't we just intuitively know the fun things to do in life?

My answer is that most of us once did. Dr. Stuart Brown in his 2010 book on play said this: "As children, we don't need instruction in how to play. We just find what we enjoy and do it."

The problem, of course, is that we grow up.

Which is a good thing. Most children are not good at completing long term projects, saving and spending money wisely—things one needs to succeed in life—things one needs to retire.

The sad part is that in doing the above, we can lose our playfulness, the ability to find fun and joy in life, the knack of being spontaneous and unself-conscious, of living in the present.

So my book is a primer on playfulness, a prompt if you like. Here are things you might want to consider doing in retirement. More importantly, they are ideas that I hope will stir your own thoughts and actions.

And in doing so, may they put a smile on your face.

One more thing—I am not a medical doctor so before taking my advice on any of the following activities, perhaps you should consult a real one, plus maybe a (pick one) psychologist, orthopedist, insurance salesperson or astrologer.

1

Write for Fun
(and Maybe Some Money, Too)

Writing a book ranks high on many retirees' want-to-do lists. So if you want to publish one, you have a lot of company. More than one million books are published every year, just in the U.S. Thus, if you find writing fun, here are some activities you might enjoy:

Take a writing class.

Search online writing classes, and you'll find many from which to choose. However, I recommend a face-to-face class, one which both teaches the fundamentals and gives you opportunity to work on your own pieces with other students. Check with your regional university, community college or city library for class offerings.

Join a writer's group.

Most cities have writers' groups. Many have specialized ones like inspirational writers or romance writers. These groups typically meet every month or two with a guest lecturer to address some aspect of writing. In addition, the group can get you in touch with people and resources you need to become a good writer.

Attend a writers' conference.

Writers' conferences feature the more successful writers/speakers. They're also valuable for the opportunities to mix with other writers for mutual help and encouragement. And most include a writers' contest to which you can submit your work and, perhaps, be rewarded with an interested agent or publisher.

Be part of a critique group.

Critique groups usually spring from formal classes or writers groups. Typically small in number (3-6), group members read and comment on each others' work. Look for people who are both insightful and encouraging and don't be afraid to change groups of it isn't a good fit.

Write for an online publication.

This works especially for nonfiction. If you write about travel or fishing and find a website that features articles on your subject, contact the webmaster to see if he or she would be interested in your work. Don't be afraid to send a small sample. And don't be discouraged with rejections. Professional authors receive more "nos" than "yeses," but they keep on submitting anyway.

Start a blog.

A writer needs readers; it's that simple. And the Internet has made it possible to find readers before you are published. So pick a niche and write short pieces on your area of interest. Look online to see the many possibilities. Also, the Web offers many free blog sites for you to get started (check out Scott Chow at the blogstarter.com). I like "take–me-along" blogs where the writer attempts a journey and takes his or her reader along for the ride. (That's how *The Best Is Yet To Be* became a book).

Publish your own book on Amazon.

It's easier than you think and not as expensive as using a do-it-yourself publisher (who will take more money and control away from you). Look online for how-to articles or, better yet, find a friend who is doing his or her print-on-demand Kindle book and has time to show you the ropes.

Write a memoir.

Memoir writing is one of the bestselling genres on Amazon, and everyone has at least one memoir in them. Besides, your great-grandkids will appreciate your life story even if you don't sell it to contemporaries. You might take a class or read a book on memoir writing, but the most important thing is to read the published memoirs that you like. Then get started. The beginning is the hardest and most important part of any book.

Create a storyboard for a novel.

Think of your novel as scenes in a movie. Get a picture of each scene in your head; then assemble them chronologically. Next write a short description of what will occur in each. Now you're ready to start your novel.

Write a back story for each of the major characters in your novel.

The back story is what happened to your characters before they entered your novel. Much of this information will not get into your book, but you need it to know how your characters will act in a given situation. Write these sketches quickly. Don't worry about grammar and spelling. Now you might want to go back and revise the storyboard.

Write a movie script.

Many people think of their novel as scenes in a movie. If you are one of these, you might consider writing a movie script. There are plenty of online classes to get you started.

Consider a graphic novel.

A graphic novel is like a comic book. It has a picture illustrating each section of text. Yet unlike a comic book, graphic novels tell the complete story with a beginning, middle and end. They should have everything a novel has, such as a building of the story, a climax and a resolution. If you like to tell a story with visuals, you should try a graphic novel. Read a few to get started. Oh, and find a good illustrator.

Try writing a children's book.

If you like to tell a story, and especially if you like to tell one to a child, you should consider writing a children's book. Again, I suggest reading several to get started. Also, you might want to tell your story to a few children first. Be sure to plan captivating illustrations and choose a good artist to render them.

Write a poem.

Poems can be short or long. They can rhyme or not rhyme. They can be funny or melancholy, light or pithy. In short, they can be anything you want them to be. Try to read (and listen) to several different kinds of verse. Pay attention to rhythm and sound. I recommend listening to spoken word poetry.

Write lyrics to a song.

Lyrics are just poetry set to music. Most will rhyme and will have the right number of syllables to fit the meter of the tune. If you are not a musician, recruit one to help you fit lyrics with music.

Try your hand at flash fiction.

According to Wikipedia, flash fiction is "a fictional work of extreme brevity that still offers character and plot development." Another source says it ranges from five to 1500 words, but no greater than 2000. Read some online examples; then see what you can do.

List ideas for a science fiction series.

If your story began with the words "A long time ago in a galaxy far, far away," what would the universe look like and who would be in charge? Become the next George Lucas and write your own vision of the future. Start now by listing possible scenarios.

Become a reviewer.

Could you write a review of a movie or book? What about the current crop of SUVs? If so, you have material for a blog, or you could find a gig writing for someone else. Try writing a few reviews and then decide what to do with them.

Write a devotional.

Do you like to study the Bible and then share your thoughts with others? If the answer is yes, you have the motivation to write devotional material, which could be shared in a blog or pitched to a religious publisher. Start now by creating two or three pieces.

Come up with an idea for a thriller or mystery.

Surely you have read a book or seen a movie that gave you an idea for a thriller or mystery. Or maybe you have observed or lived a life event that could be made into a story. List some ideas in your journal; then create a storyboard from the best of them.

Construct a travel narrative.

It makes sense that if travel is the number one leisure activity of retired baby boomers (and it is), then writing about travel will give you a huge audience. Start now with a trip firmly etched in your memory or keep a journal during your next outing. Remember, your audience wants not only vivid description but story and reflection. What obstacles did you (or someone else) face? What thoughts came to you in your journey? Was there an epiphany?

Write a how-to book.

Everyone is an expert in something. What do you know that would be helpful to a novice? Would you enjoy helping others accomplish something? Instruction books sell well on Amazon. Take a look at some and decide what isn't there that you could provide, or that you could do better. Start looking today.

Write an editorial.

Are you passionate about thoughts and practices that affect everyday people? Do you wish you could share your thoughts with a wider audience? Then start with a letter to the editor in a publication you read. Be sure to read the guidelines (if they are listed) or look at other letters for an idea of length and tone. If the publication likes your stuff, they may contact you about future pieces.

Write a short story.

Short stories have a plot, setting and characters like a novel, but everything is constrained by time —both the amount of words that can be put in them and the amount of time (minutes, hours, days as opposed to years) during which the story takes place. Often they will start with a climax and work backwards toward plot and resolution. Read a few; then try your own.

Or try this: write a short story in four or five paragraphs.
1. In a long paragraph, develop a protagonist for a story.
2. In one or two paragraphs, place your protagonist in a scary or untenable situation.
3. In the next paragraph, raise the stakes. Make the situation more scary, more untenable.
4. In a final paragraph, let the story reach a climax and begin to resolve the conflict.

Develop a series of nostalgic pieces.

Readers love nostalgia. Try thinking of one event in your early years (first bicycle, first friend, first kiss); then write a short piece (500-600 words) about it. This could become an entry in your blog or you could combine it with others to make a memoir.

Come up with an idea for historical fiction.

Do you wonder how real people experienced the events of the past, people who didn't make it into history books? Why not create that person and tell his or her story in a novel? You can start today by creating a storyboard and back stories of your characters.

Write a love story.

Love stories don't have to be "boy meets girl." How about a girl who falls for a wild mustang or a boy who is seduced by the open sea? There are thousands of love stories waiting to be written. Maybe one of them is in your head. Start today with a storyboard.

Tell a story through letters, emails or texts.

Do you suppose you could see only the texts people sent one another and, from that, piece together a story? What if you also had texts from some of their friends and family? You could then add to the story with narration or leave it alone (texts only) and let the readers' imagination come up with plot and resolution.

Write about sports or music or art or . . .

What is your passion? You will write best if you know the answer to that question. Write about what interests you, and you will interest your audience. It's that easy. Take time to brainstorm (and write down) some of those interests. Then write an article for a blog. Hint: you can make it an editorial. "If the Broncos want to capture another Super Bowl, here's what they need to do."

Finally, try these writing prompts for fun.

Following are some of the prompts I used in my college creative writing classes. For each, start with the prompt and then write for 10-15 minutes nonstop. If you are writing long hand (and I suggest it) do not let the pen or pencil stop moving. If you can't think of anything, write "and then, and then," over and over until you get started again.

Time warps, time machines, parallel universes—all nonsense, stuff for people with histrionic personalities and overactive imaginations. Anyway, I thought so, until the day I _____.

You are sitting in a coffee shop working on a writing project and notice a person in the parking lot (give description—age, gender, other characteristics—what he or she is doing). This person enters the building and either asks you or you feel compelled to offer her something to eat or drink. As the person begins her meal, she shares her story. What does she say?

I'm a predictable person. Every day, I get up at the same time, eat the same breakfast, drive the same car into work—along the same route. Until yesterday. Such a small change. Such a big consequence. . . . (continue story)

"Do something," my mind yelled at my body. But what? I didn't know. I did know Clark Kent wasn't going to suddenly show up. If someone rescued us, that someone would be me. And I knew something else, something that troubled me even more: I'd have to face my greatest fear to pull it off. (continue story)

I pinched myself to make sure I wasn't dreaming. Ouch! Yes, this was the Rose Garden. Yes, that was the President speaking just a few feet in front of where I sat. And, yes, he was introducing me. As he talked, time seemed to stop as my mind replayed the last 48 hours. (Where had you been? What did you do? Why were you here?)

Faded and crinkled at the edges, the envelope had my name on it alright, but the postmark, which I could barely make out, read September 1, 1985. Wow—25 years and one week ago! I examined the return address, also faded and hard to read. Might it be? Could it be? My fingers shook as I gently slipped the opener under the edges, made a clean cut and looked at the familiar cursive before me. Modify the dates and time if you want; then, write the letter. Who wrote the letter? Why? What did he/she say?

The captain had announced our arrival, and flight attendants were making sure our belts were buckled and seats were in an upright position—it all seemed so normal—except for the destination. Yep, after all these years, I was finally landing in _____ (continue story).

One more thing:

I had students go to a busy library or coffee shop with computer or writing materials in hand. They were to select someone there (hopefully, several chairs away) and write his or her story. Where did they come from? Where were they going? Add a lot of detail. What was their family of origin like? Who was their best friend in elementary school? Now? How about her favorite color, movie star, sports team, food? You get the idea. Who knows? You might get a novel out of this. Just be discreet (you also might get arrested).

2

Do It on the Water

Did you know that 71% of the Earth's surface is covered with water? Did you know that the United States has over 250,000 rivers stretching a total of 3.5 million miles? And then there's nearly 100,000 miles of coastal shoreline (along the Atlantic, Pacific, Gulf of Mexico and Great Lakes). With all that water, there just has to be a bunch of fun to be had on and around it. Here are my suggestions:

Stay on the water.

Choose a fancy motel or vacation rental by owner (Vrbo) with an ocean view (off-season rates can be pretty affordable) or rent a mountain cabin next to a trout stream. Or, literally, stay on the water (I found a two-bedroom, one-bath houseboat on the Columbia River for $89 per night).

Explore your favorite lake in a motor boat.

You can get a 23' Pontoon Boat for $550 per day at Lake Powell (on the Colorado River near Page, AZ). Or add some risk and fun and rent a jet ski ($359 per day at Lake Powell).

Learn to sail.

The American Sailing Association claims to have the largest group of sailing schools in the world, and you can choose from locations like Honolulu, HI or Seward, AK. Or, for a less extreme (and expensive) experience, check out the YMCA in a city next to a lake or ocean (greater Charlotte, NC offers classes for beginners).

Paddle a canoe.

Pretend you're Daniel Boone and learn to paddle a canoe. Located on the Ouiska Chitto Creek near Oberlin, LA, White Sand Canoe Rental will let you out and pick you up from this scenic waterway (about a nine-mile, 4-6 hour trip). Overnight trips are also available. Oh, and they offer senior citizen discounts.

You don't have to go to remote locations to canoe. Check out beautiful Tempe Town Lake in the greater Phoenix area where I found more than half a dozen boat rental companies.

Row, row, row your boat.

You can rent a row boat for $10 per hour in the Netherlands, $6 per hour in Latvia, or $97 a day in Sweden. Or stay in the U.S. where $150 will get you a whole week at Umbagog Lake State Park in New Hampshire.

Kayak on a sea or lake.

Most U.S. lakes, big and small, rent kayaks, a popular activity, especially among seniors. On the other hand, a sea kayak or touring kayak is a vessel developed for paddling on open waters of lakes, bays and the ocean. These are designed for higher cruising speed, cargo capacity, ease of straight-line paddling and comfort for long journeys. You'll need a lesson for sea kayaking so check out kayakacademy.com in Washington state.

Water ski or wake board.

Water skiing and wake boarding are more pricey, but for enthusiasts they are well worth it. Sneaky Pete's on Lake Lewisville north of Dallas rents a 21′ deluxe ski boat that will hold 10 (the price is $520 for four hours, $960 for eight).

Fulfill your surfing fantasy.

Live near a beach with good waves? With a little conditioning, a surf lesson and practice, a coach in Oceanside, CA says he can teach you to ride a wave in no time.

Plunge into some white water.

How about taking a whitewater rafting trip down the Arkansas River? The folks at Noah's Ark north of Salida, CO can give you a once-in-a-lifetime experience for well under $100.

Take a float trip.

Want a more relaxing experience? The people at River Ranch Resort near Springfield, IL say inner tubes are the old-school way to float a river, in this case, a five-mile section of the Missouri. At $25 per tube per day, you won't go broke on this one.

Enjoy an ocean cruise.

If you are one of the 25.3 million who cruised globally in 2019, I don't need to say anything more. You know the contagious pleasure the big ships offer. There's a reason the cruise industry is the fastest-growing category in the leisure travel market. Simply pick your line and your destination.

Choose a river cruise.

Experience a short cruise, maybe on a giant paddle wheeler or luxury yacht (Lake Tahoe) or experience a 19th century big wheel, steam driven paddle wheeler on the Mississippi (check out the *General Jackson* on the Cumberland River near Nashville).

Or for a more extensive experience

Investigate Viking River Cruises for international travel (with destinations like Vienna and Budapest on the Danube or Amsterdam, Cologne and Basel on the Rhine). For domestic rivers, American River Cruises claims to be the leader. I like descriptions of their trips on the Mississippi, Columbia and Snake.

Take a fishing trip.

There are so many options for this one, from a guided hunt for King Salmon in Alaska to a trip to a city park in, say, Oklahoma City (which has a rainbow trout season). And fishing trips are always special with grandkids.

Go deep-sea fishing.

If you haven't done it before, try deep sea fishing. You'll want to book a charter boat for this. It's pricey, but not so much when you split it between fishing buddies. Then try your luck with marlin or tuna off the coast of Charleston, SC, or mahi-mahi in the Florida Keys, or Red Snapper in the Gulf of Mexico near Port Aransas, TX or King Salmon in Puget Sound off the coast of Washington. Oh, and if you opt for the Keys, one boat offers Captain Dan himself as your guide.

Learn to fly fish and then try out your new skills in a picturesque spot.

First, watch *A River Runs through It* with Brad Pitt. Next take a fly fishing class (a number of Osher Institute of Lifelong Learning schools offer one, including the campus at Carnegie Mellon). Then if you like fly fishing for trout, I recommend a float trip down the San Juan near Farmington, NM. Or if you prefer to strap on waders and stand in a more shallow river, try the Rio Grande north of South Fork, CO. And these scenic spots are not all in the Rockies. Try Rock Creek in the Chattahoochee National Forest of North Georgia.

If it's bass you want, my sources say the best bass fishing lakes are Santee Cooper Lakes in South

Carolina or Sacramento San Joaquin Delta in California or Lake Fork in Texas. Bass lovers seem to split between fly fishing and lures, but you can still use the real thing—night crawlers, minnows or crawdads.

Or you can return to a simpler time. For me, that would be fishing with a cane pole and bobber on Palo Duro Creek. The fish of my childhood were bluegill perch and mudcat, and the bait was canned corn, worms or whatever was left of Mom's Vienna sausage sandwich.

Campout next to a trout stream.

Not only are trout one of the best fighting fish to reel in, the sound of a gurgling stream will cure the most resistant insomnia. I like the headwaters of the Rio Grande north of Creede, CO (check out North Clear Creek Falls campground).

Enjoy a River Walk.

Several U.S. cities have elaborately designed river walks with opportunities to shop, dine, walk or bike along them. And in many you can see them from the river itself in a tour boat. Make a list of five or six to put on your bucket list. I suggest San Antonio, Chicago, Milwaukee, Reno, Oklahoma City and Three Rivers Heritage Trail in Pittsburgh.

Swim when and where you can.

If you love to swim, but building your own pool is too much for the budget, then consider the alternatives. Health clubs and planned communities often have pools, and your schedule will allow you to choose times when there's no crowd. Also, local colleges have pools, and many offer special activities like water aerobics for seniors.

Or you might consider a swim vacation. Find a hotel near a beach or lake during the low season. Or find a four- or five-star hotel with an amazing pool and go there during non-peak times of the year. Phoenix temps often reach 110+ during August, which makes hotel rooms cheap, and if you swim early, you'll avoid the heat and the crowd.

And there's always the hot tub.

If you don't want the expense and maintenance of a pool, hot tubs have a pleasure all their own (think long, hot baths). And did you know soaking in a hot tub not only relaxes your muscles and helps you sleep, it burns calories (not a lot, but, hey, calories are calories)?

3

Intended for Pleasure

In 1872, when Congress established *Yellowstone Park* in the Montana and Wyoming territories, they dubbed this first national park "a public park or pleasuring-ground for the benefit and enjoyment of the people."

I like that; don't you? Our first national park (and, by precedent, all the others) was created and intended for pleasure. It seems to me that makes each eligible for the fun-things-to-do list of retirees. So I'll start my suggestions with the 10 most visited sites.

With 12.5 million visitors, the *Great Smoky Mountain National Park* in Tennessee was the most visited in 2019. Put it on your travel list and don't miss Dollywood and the Island at Pigeon Forge during your stay. By the way, I'm using 2019 numbers because 2020 data was skewed due to the pandemic, and 2021 is not yet available.

Coming in at number two (5.97 million visitors), the *Grand Canyon* offers 1.2 million acres of stunning desert views. I recommend staying on the south rim at a lodge in the Village, and while there, hiking at least some of the Bright Angel and/ or North Kaibab Trail.

The third most visited park (4.7 million visitors) was *Rocky Mountain National Park* near Estes Park, CO. Be sure to travel the Rocky Mountain Trail Ridge Road—the highest continuous paved road in the United States. Mountain views don't get any more spectacular.

At number four (4.5 million visitors), *Zion National Park* in Utah also offers amazing canyon views. In addition to a plethora of hiking choices, you'll want to drive along the Zion Canyon Scenic Drive.

California's *Yosemite National Park* was the fifth most visited (4.4 million visitors). The large granite formation known as El Capitan (which rises 3,000 feet from base to summit) rates as one of the most familiar natural formations in the U.S. Perhaps you will enjoy it most by looking skyward as you float down the slow moving Merced River in an inflatable raft.

Number six on the 2019 most visited park list (4 million visitors) was *Yellowstone,* whose 2.2 million acres lie in three different states (Idaho, Wyoming and Montana). Of course, you'll want to see Old Faithful and Yellowstone Falls. Stay away from the grizzlies and buffalo (the latter harm more people than the bears).

Acadia National Park in Maine came in at number seven (3.4 million visitors). Everyone talks about the beautiful scenery and the carriage roads, which you'll want to travel on a bicycle since automobiles are prohibited.

Less than 100 miles south of Yellowstone is the *Grand Teton National Park,* which was the eighth most visited (3.4 million visitors). The Tetons are famous for their jagged mountain peaks, beautiful scenery (you have to see Jenny Lake) and wildlife viewing (you'll travel far to see more elk and moose).

And don't miss Jackson Hole, WY on your way out. Jackson Hole is famous for its shops, restaurants, and notable celebrities who call it home. Kanye West and Kim Kardashian, Harrison Ford, Sandra Bullock, Brad Pitt, Tiger Woods and Matthew McConaughe have second homes there.

At number nine (3.2 million visitors), Washington's *Olympic National Park* boasts excellent boating, fishing and hiking, all in a lush rain forest.

Rounding out the top 10 (3 million visitors) was Montana's *Glacier National Park* with glacier-carved peaks and valleys running to the Canadian border. You'll want to view the sites from the mountainous Going-to-the-Sun Road, which traverses the park.

These are the most visited parks (or were in 2019), but looking at a list of the others (pull it up for yourself online), there is plenty of fun still to be had. For instance, take a look at these:

Lying in the crater of an extinct volcano, *Crater Lake* is the deepest and—with that deep blue color—some say the prettiest lake in the U.S. Visitors can bicycle the 33 miles around the lake, yet, according to concessioner Crater Lake Hospitality, the best way to view this national park is on a boat tour. The only hitch? You have to descend nearly 700' in a little over a mile to reach the boat dock.

Oh, and you'll have to ascend the same distance to get back to your car.

If nothing else, I would go to *Sequoia National Park* to see the world's largest tree (yep, I said world's largest). Dubbed the General Sherman, this redwood stands nearly 175' high and is 36.5' in diameter at the base.

Almost 1,000 miles north of Sequoia, *Mount Rainer* dominates the Washington landscape. Boasting more glacier cover than any other peak in the lower 48, the park offers many fun hiking trails, but the one to the top (14,410') is not for amateurs.

Also not for the amateur is North America's highest peak, 20,310 foot Mt. McKinley, which is located in *Denali National Park* in Alaska. I hope you get to view it on a day when the clouds don't hide the summit. Oh, and be sure to visit nearby Talkeetna, the small, somewhat quirky, Alaska town which inspired the TV show *Northern Exposure*.

By the way, not only does Denali boast the highest peak in the U.S., at 6.1 million acres, it is the third largest national park. In fact, seven of the top 10 largest U.S. parks are in Alaska. Of them, Denali, Kenai Fjords, Wrangell-St. Elias and Glacier Bay are the most accessible to tourists. At an astonishing 13.2 million acres, Wrangell-St. Elias is the largest. But, for my money, I would visit *Glacier Bay*, which is home to massive calving glaciers and humpback whales. You'll have to take a helicopter or cruise ship to get there, which, in my view, is another perk.

The largest park in the lower 48 is Death Valley (3.4 million acres), followed by Yellowstone (2.2 million) and Everglades National Park in Florida (1.5 million).

Death Valley is known for its extremes—North America's driest and hottest spot (2.2 inches of rainfall annually and a high of 134°F recorded in 1913). At 282' below sea level, it's also the lowest spot on the continent. Why would anyone want to visit such a harsh climate? Fans point to the absence of city lights, which makes for excellent star gazing, and the austere desert beauty, which has made it a movie set for nearly 100 films.

You go from 2.2 inches of precipitation per year at Death Valley to 56 inches at *Everglades National Park* in Florida where you can view Sandhill cranes, flamingos and several types of herons, along with another 350 bird species in their natural habitat. Be careful; there are also panthers in the glades.

Returning to a description of western parks (not a bad idea since 40 of the 63 national parks are in the West), I come back to an earlier post. I wrote that the sequoia redwoods, close to Fresno, CA are the largest trees in the world. And they are, but they are not the tallest. That would be their cousins to the north and west, the coastal California redwoods that are more slender and tall (can reach heights over 370'—that's 37 stories). By the way, these coastal redwoods have their answer to the General Sherman of Sequoia. It's called Hyperion after the titan of Greek mythology and stands 380' tall.

Redwood National Park in northern California is host to these beauties, along with the largest herd of Roosevelt Elk in the world. And speaking of large, Roosevelt bulls can weigh 1,100 pounds, the largest elk in North America.

Staying in California (and why not? the state has the most national parks at nine), *Channel Islands National Park* is located just off the coast near Ventura. These five small islands offer snorkeling, diving, kayaking and hiking in an uncrowded environment one would not expect so close to greater Los Angeles. You can get there only by ferry or private boat and must take along your own food and water. This is not for the fainthearted. Visitors to the common unloading port at Santa Cruz Island must climb from the boat up a steel-rung ladder to a dock, and then climb 157 stairs to the top of the island.

Known for its 2,000 sandstone arches, *Arches National Park* lies just north of Moab, Utah. Take the 19-mile scenic drive for formations like Balanced Rock, the Window, Double Arch and Delicate Arch.

Nearby to Arches sits *Canyonlands National Park*. Known for its massive rock pinnacles and rugged canyons, the park contains hundreds of miles of four-wheel drive roads ideal for ATVs and mountain bikes. Just stay out of Salt Creek in Peekaboo Horse Canyon, where, according to the park website, you might encounter deep sand, deep water and quicksand. Quicksand?

Go southwest of Canyonlands, and you'll come to *Bryce Canyon National Park*. Pull up an online picture of the Bryce Canyon Amphitheater (a natural semi circle of dramatic, sandstone pinnacles), and you'll know why you need to visit this park.

Great Basin National Park is in eastern Nevada near the Utah border. Like Death Valley, the absence of artificial light makes the area perfect for star gazing. Take the Wheeler Peak Scenic Drive (12 miles of paved, but steep and winding road) and observe the plentiful lakes, streams and wildlife.

As you would expect, the *Petrified Forest National Park* in northeastern Arizona is filled with colorful petrified wood (the world's largest deposits). It will take less than an hour to drive the park's 48-mile road, which includes a section of the Painted Desert, but you will want to spend plenty of time stopping at the many viewpoints along the way.

If it's ancient Native American cliff dwellings you want, then *Mesa Verde* in southwestern Colorado is one of the best preserved. On your way there, stop at The Chapin Mesa Archeological Museum. You won't be disappointed.

For a pristine picture of the Old West, in all its remoteness and ruggedness, you will do no better than the *Theodore Roosevelt National Park* in western North Dakota. Take the 90-minute scenic loop drive and enjoy the wild horses, bearded bison, elk and prairie dogs. Warning: there is no food, lodging, gas, auto repair or mail service in the park.

If you want to overlook a ruggedly beautiful, dramatic and sheer canyon precipice, then you need to stand on the edge of the *Black Canyon of the Gunnison* in western Colorado. The park has several scenic trails along both the north and south rims, but if you want to descend almost 3,000' to the Gunnison River, you are on your own. There are no maintained or marked trails. Which means, according to the park website, "hikers are expected to find their own way and be prepared for self-rescue." Self-rescue? Scary, huh?

The *Great Sand Dunes National Park* in southern Colorado hosts the tallest sand dunes in North America. The most striking is Star Dune, which reaches a dizzying 755'. Visitors climb and explore, and they "sand board" and "sand sled." Seriously. You can rent the necessary apparatuses in nearby Alamosa.

For more desert scenery, *Big Bend National Park* in Texas encompasses the largest protected area of Chihuahuan Desert in the United States (over 800,000 acres). I suggest staying just outside the park at the Gage Hotel in Marathon. Once the headquarters of a large Texas ranch, the setting will make you think you've entered a John Wayne movie.

If you've never seen a Joshua tree, you might stop reading and pull up a picture on the Internet. They look like a tree, having a long single trunk with five or six thick branches at the top. But look closer. The branches end in spiky clumps that look much like a yucca plant. And they are. The botanical name for Joshua tree is yucca brevifolia. Anyway, *Joshua Tree National Park* in southern California features 800,000 acres of the plant, plus other captivating desert scenery.

If you like caves, you'll love *Carlsbad Caverns* in southeastern New Mexico. This labyrinth of nearly 100 caves has one called the Big Room, which is 4,000' long, 625' wide and 255' high. Visitors are blown away by the stalagmites (mineral columns rising from the cave floor, which can look like needles, flowers or even popcorn), and stalactites (the same material hanging like icicles from the roof). I suggest entering through the mile long foot path and taking the elevators back up.

When you leave Carlsbad, drive west for about 150 miles to *White Sands National Park*, famous for its 145,000 acres of pure white sand dunes, and next to the Department of Defense's White Sands Missile Range, which according to their website, is the largest "fully-instrumented open air range" in the U.S. I think that means you need to stay on approved roads or something bad will happen to you.

Moving back to the middle of the country, *Gateway Arch National Park*, located in St. Louis, celebrates the starting point of the Lewis and Clark

Expedition. Of course, the main attraction is the towering 630' arch, designed by architect Eero Saarinen, an amazing man who never received a college degree. The website says I can best enjoy the panoramic view by riding to the top in a kind of tram (which one visitor describes as "rickety"). No thank you.

If you are interested in the old Erie Canal, Ohio's *Cuyahoga Valley National Park* features a restored section of the original tow path. While there, visit Brandywine Falls, a picturesque, 60' falls with views from an upper and lower board-walk. The round-trip hike is about five miles from the Boston Mill Visitor Center, but my map shows a shorter trip (1.5 miles each way) from an unpaved parking lot at the Stanford Trailhead.

Staying in the Midwest, *Isle Royale National Park* in Michigan is a group of islands in Lake Superior near the border with Canada. No vehicles are allowed in this land of forests, lakes, moose and wolves. Yes, wolves. The gray wolf has roamed the area since the late 1940s when they are thought to have crossed an ice bridge from the Canadian mainland.

And the Midwest also has its sand dunes. *Indiana Dunes National Park* lies along 20 miles of the southern shore of Lake Michigan. It is one of the newest national parks, receiving the official designation in February of 2019.

Eighteen miles southeast of the South Carolina capital at Columbia lies the state's only national park. *Congaree National Park* has the largest old growth hardwood forest left in the U.S. These trees provide an unusually high canopy, which supports a large population of birds, including eight species of woodpeckers. In fact, some ornithologists contend that the ivory-billed woodpecker, thought to be extinct since the 1940s, lives on at Congaree.

The eastern U.S. has its share of whitewater, too. Check out the *New River Gorge National Park*, 70,000 acres along West Virginia's New River, which became a national park in December of 2020. For everything from family rafting to class five whitewater, search the Internet for Adventures on the Gorge.

For fall foliage, check out Skyline Drive in Virginia's *Shenandoah National Park*, a scenic highway winding through the top country of the Blue Ridge Mountains. There are over 75 breathtaking overlooks.

Located in north central Maryland, *Catoctin Mountain Park* is known, not for what it offers the public—25 miles of hiking trails—but for what it withholds from the public. The presidential retreat created by FDR and known as Camp David is off-limits to visitors. Here the Normandy invasion was planned, the entrance into and withdrawal from Vietnam were discussed and the Camp David Accords between Israel and Egypt were signed.

Without doubt the highest concentration of properties administered by the National Park Service can be found in and around Washington, DC. Following is a list:

- Belmont-Paul Women's Equality National Monument
- Carter G. Woodson Home National Historic Site
- Chesapeake and Ohio Canal National Historical Park
- Constitution Gardens
- Ford's Theatre National Historic Site
- Franklin D. Roosevelt Memorial
- Frederick Douglass National Historic Site
- George Washington Memorial Parkway
- Korean War Veterans Memorial
- Lincoln Memorial

- Lyndon Baines Johnson Memorial Grove on the Potomac
- Martin Luther King, Jr. Memorial
- Mary McLeod Bethune Council House National Historic Site
- National Capital Parks
- National Mall
- Pennsylvania Avenue National Historic Site
- Rock Creek Park
- Theodore Roosevelt Island
- Thomas Jefferson Memorial
- Vietnam Veterans Memorial
- Washington Monument
- White House
- World War I Memorial
- World War II Memorial

Before you get started, and if you aren't already familiar with DC, I have a suggestion. Visit it with someone who is, which is what we did in 2017. Insiders know how to get around quickly, where to eat and stay, which places to visit first and at what time of day, and, most importantly, they have access to people who can give private tours of the Congress and White House.

That's important (the insider). I also suggest that you take your time and enjoy the experience. Choose quality over quantity, meaning don't make this a contest of how many things you can cram into a limited amount of time. Do I sound like I'm preaching? I am. To me (yep, there's a story, but it's too long to share here).

Besides national parks there are 129 national monuments, 20 national preserves, 61 national historical parks and 87 national historic sites. And then there are state parks, 10,234 by one count. My state of Texas has over 80, and if that sounds like a lot, eleven states have more than 100. California leads us all with 270.

So my point is that travel is one of our greatest joys in retirement, and, pandemic restrictions not withstanding, there are hundreds, maybe thousands of fun places to enjoy without leaving the good ol' U.S. of A.

22 Must-See National Monuments

Admiralty Island, Alaska—densest population of brown bears in U.S.

Bandalier, New Mexico—ancestral Pueblo rock paintings.

Booker T. Washington, Virginia—birthplace of African American legend

Canyon de Chelly, Arizona—picturesque home of the Navajo

Chimney Rock, Colorado—historic landmark in San Juan Mountains

Devil's Tower, Wyoming—stunning rock formation, was first national monument (1906)

Fort McHenry, Maryland—defended Baltimore in War of 1812

Fort Stanwix, New York—resisted 1777 British siege

Fort Union, New Mexico—frontier military post on old Santa Fe Trail

Governor's Island, New York—Army post in New York Harbor from 1783 to 1966

Grand Portage, Minnesota—8.5 mile footpath bypasses waterfalls on Pigeon River

Harriet Tubman Underground Railroad, Maryland—celebrates famous savior of thousands of escaping slaves

Jewel's Cave, South Dakota—fifth largest cave in the world, runs beneath Black Hills

Little Big Horn Battlefield, Montana—George Armstrong Custer defeated by Sitting Bull and Crazy Horse (1876)

Misty Fjords, Alaska—called Yosemite of the North

Montezuma Castle, Arizona—cliff dwellings dating from 1100 AD

Mount Rushmore, South Dakota—60′ high granite sculpture of presidents Washington, Jefferson, Lincoln and T. Roosevelt (technically, a national *memorial*)

Muir Woods, California—protects one of the last stands of old growth Coastal Redwoods

Natural Bridges, Utah—second and third largest natural land bridges in western hemisphere

Pearl Harbor, Hawaii—commemorates the attack that brought U.S. into World War II (technically, a national *memorial*)

Rainbow Bridge, Utah—one of the world's largest land bridges

Statue of Liberty—a gift from France in 1886, celebrates U.S. independence

National Historic Sites and National Historical Parks

Since there are so many of these, I'm not going to list them for you; however, you can get a full list here: https://en.wikipedia.org/wiki/National_Historic_Site_(United_States)

On these lists you will find birth places of most of the presidents and other influential leaders (like MLK). And there are many old forts and places that figured prominently in U.S. history. Remember, the point of my lists is fun things to do. I consider visiting historic places fun, but not everyone will. So look at the lists. If you find something that piques your interest, click on it and do your own research (that's part of the fun).

31 of the Best State Parks

I'm pretty sure state parks, like their national cousins, are intended for pleasure. So if one or several of these seem a good prospect for fun, look them up, do the research and plan a visit. Happy hunting.

Tettegouche State Park, Minnesota—View Minnesota's highest falls and others along the Baptism River.

Iao Valley State Park, Hawaii—Hey, it's in a rain forest.

Eldorado Canyon State Park, Colorado—Enjoy hiking and mountain biking in Boulder's backyard.

Niagara Falls State Park, New York—It's the oldest state park in the U.S. Be sure to "explore the roar" on the *Maid of Mist* boat tour.

Baxter State Park, Maine—Enjoy day hikes, canoes, kayaks and fishing, all on 200,000 acres of park land.

Kachemak Bay State Park—This was Alaska's first state park, and with 400,000 acres, Kachemak Bay has all things Alaskan.

Anza-Borrego Desert State Park, California—Boasting 650,000 desert acres, it's the largest state park in the lower 48.

Makoshika State Park, Montana—In the badlands of Montana, this park has 11,000 acres of vistas and hiking.

Smith Rock State Park, Oregon—A U.S. Cavalry soldier named Smith fell to his death here during a battle with the Northern Paiute in 1863. Be careful where you step.

Little Missouri State Park, North Dakota—Described as a "quiet oasis," this park runs through the badlands.

Emerald Bay State Park, California—Part of Lake Tahoe, Emerald Bay is known for its striking blue-green hue.

Slide Rock State Park, Arizona—Enjoy a natural water slide in Oak Creek Canyon just north of Sedona.

Letchworth State Park, New York—Called the Grand Canyon of the East, the park features 17 miles of deep gorge with several waterfalls. White water rafting is available (hopefully, you won't go over the falls).

Dead Horse Point State Park, Utah—Next to Canyonlands National Park, Dead Horse Point boasts stunning overviews (yes, there is a story behind the name, but it's too long to share here).

Peninsula State Park, Wisconsin—The park contains eight miles of scenic Green Bay shoreline, from Kayak to Horseshoe Island.

Cayo Costa State Park, Florida—This island south of Boca Grande is accessible by boat or helicopter.

Cathedral Gorge State Park, Nevada—The park is known for stunning sandstone formations, hiking trails and slot canyons.

Chugach State Park, Alaska—Encompassing 500,000 pristine acres east of Anchorage, the park is home to over 60 glaciers, and, yep, there are bears.

Fall Creek Falls State Park, Tennessee—The park features a 256' falls and provides hiking, boating and a ropes course.

Hunting Island State Park, South Carolina—This 5,000-acre barrier island boasts more than one million visitors a year.

Adirondack Park, New York—The park is known for canoe routes, skiing, snowboarding and spectacular fall foliage.

Custer State Park, South Dakota—Located near Mount Rushmore in the Black Hills, the park is known for its views of bison, wild burros and beautiful lakes.

Julia Pfeiffer Burns State Park, California—This park features 300' high redwoods, some 2500 years old. Also, the area touches the coast at Big Sur.

Palo Duro Canyon State Park, Texas—The park sits in the second largest canyon in the U.S. Come in the summer and enjoy the musical drama "TEXAS" in a colorful amphitheater.

Na Pali Coast State Park, Hawaii—You'll see towering sea cliffs and cascading waterfalls on Kauai Island.

Goblin Valley State Park, Utah—The park is named for the mushroom-shaped sandstone pinnacles that look like goblins.

Chimney Rock State Park, North Carolina—The rock's spectacular granite face was the backdrop for the movie, *Last of the Mohicans*.

Castle Rocks State Park, Idaho—The area is world famous for rock climbing.

Island Beach State Park, New Jersey—The area features 10 miles of sandy beach on a skinny barrier peninsula.

Palouse Falls State Park, Washington—The park contains a thundering 198′ waterfall but has limited tent camping.

Porcupine Mountains Wilderness State Park—With 60,000 acres bordering Lake Superior, the park has four scenic waterfalls.

Of course, all these places need to be accessed. So perhaps you need to discover the fun of getting there. Turn the page.

4

The Fun of Getting There

Ten years ago I was seduced by a train whistle. Sounding low and mournful as I sat outside alone on a Sunday morning, it called me back to a childhood fascination with trains, a belief that whatever lay along those tracks was beautiful, adventuresome, even magical.

So a few months later, Charlotte and I drove to Albuquerque to begin what we labeled our Great Western Train Ride. In five days we would take Amtrak 5,742 miles, from Albuquerque to Los Angeles, Los Angeles to Seattle, Seattle to Chicago and back to Albuquerque. That's five days and nights on the train, plus another four in hotels along the way.

And we learned something important about travel. Sometimes the greatest joy lies not in the destination but in getting there—in the choice of transportation (like a train) that is an adventure in itself. That's what this chapter is all about.

Amtrak's Most Scenic

If you're new to Amtrak, there are a few things you need to know up front. One, planes can be late a few minutes; trains, a few hours or more. So schedule plenty of time for changing from one train to another. Often after a long route, we spent an overnight in a hotel and caught the next train in the morning.

Two, there's a lot of difference between coach and a sleeper berth. Put succinctly, with a sleeper you are treated like a queen or king (privacy, preference in the dining car, your own attendant to see to your needs); coach is more like riding a bus. You are on your own.

But whether you choose a roomette or a larger family room, sleepers are expensive (like a ritzy hotel). So, my suggestion is to take coach for a short trip and a sleeper if you're going to be onboard overnight. Either way, the scenery can make it magical. Following are some passenger favorites on Amtrak:

Adirondack—a 10-hour trip from NYC to Montreal. Sit back and enjoy the wine country of the Hudson Valley.

Sunset Limited—48 hours, New Orleans to Los Angeles via Tucson and Phoenix. Experience bayou country, Texas ranches and the southwestern desert.

Southwest Chief—40 hours, Chicago to LA via Albuquerque and Flagstaff. Cross the mighty Mississippi; then see wheat fields, mountains and deserts, all part of the great American West.

California Zephyr—Emeryville, California (next to Oakland) to Chicago, 51 hours. Crosses both the Sierra Nevada and Rocky Mountain Ranges. Scenery doesn't get much better than that.

Texas Eagle—33 hours, Chicago to San Antonio through Dallas and Austin. See the land of Lincoln, the Arkansas Ozarks and the piney woods of East Texas.

Coast Starlight—a 35-hour run from Los Angeles to Seattle. Views are of lush valleys, towering forests, the Pacific shoreline and high mountains.

Amtrak Cascades—11-hour route from Vancouver, BC through Seattle, across the Columbia River Gorge at the Oregon line and ending at Eugene, OR. Best way to experience the Pacific Northwest.

Empire Builder—Chicago to Seattle through Glacier National Park in Montana. Experience the splendor of the American West.

Pacific Surfliner—6-hour trip from San Luis Obispo to San Diego. Discover the cities and coastline of Southern California.

Lake Shore Limited—a 19-hour route between Chicago and New York City. You'll pass the southern shore of Lake Michigan, the Mohawk River and the Erie Canal with views of some of the prettiest shorelines in America.

Downeaster—3-hour, 25-minute ride from Brunswick, ME to Boston, MA. Enjoy historic colonial cities and the captivating scenery of northern New England. There are five round-trips daily.

Maple Leaf—12-hour, 30-minute route from NYC to Toronto, Canada. Enjoy views of New York's wine country, the Hudson Valley and Niagra Falls.

Cardinal, but stopping at White Sulphur Springs—Part of the route from NYC to Chicago (west from NYC to White Sulfur Springs, WV). View the Blue Ridge and Allegheny Mountains and the beautiful Shenandoah valley.

Scenic Railroads

Unlike Amtrak routes, trains designated as Scenic Railroads are not intended to take you from point A to point B, but to give you a pleasurable "scenic" experience. The U.S. has many of these, and I've included most in this list. For descriptions, I've relied heavily on customer reviews.

Blue Ridge Scenic Railway—4 hours, including 2-hour layover at McCaysville, GA and Copperhill, TN. Reviewers liked the hosts/narrators, open cars and touring the destination villages. They advise you to eat before you shop because restaurants fill up quickly.

Cape Cod Central Railroad—2½ hour dinner train on Cape Cod, MA. Reviewers were not impressed with the scenery (obscured by trees and brush), but were greatly impressed with the 5-course meal and beverages. The Platinum Gold Car seems to be the way to go.

Cass Scenic Railroad—features a choice of several vintage locomotives and destinations. The long, uphill haul to Bald Knob takes about 4½ hours for the 22-mile round trip. The only railroad to have its own accompanying state park, Cass has a theater, museum and on-site accommodations in a restored "company house." Reviewers love the place: "To say I fell in love with Cass would be a huge understatement."

Cumbres & Toltec Scenic Railroad—Billed as America's longest and highest narrow-gauge railway still in operation, the C&TSR travels 64 miles between Chama, NM and Antonito, CO. Beginning at either end, passengers travel one-way to the destination and return by bus. Reviewers give it an A+ for scenery (hillsides, valleys and mountains).

Cuyahoga Valley Scenic Railroad—Operating in concert with Cuyahoga Valley National Park, this railroad seems to be liked best for its connection with the park and Akron, OH. Reviewers give it low ratings for scenery ("not a good way to see the park"), but bicycle enthusiasts love its connections with a bike trail, where they can disembark and continue on their own bikes (which the train carries for them).

Durango & Silverton Narrow Gauge Railroad— This 45-mile, 4½ hour excursion travels along the Animas River between Durango and Silverton, CO. Passengers disembark in the high, one-time mining town of Silverton for touristy shops and several good dining options. Reviewers rave about the beauty of the San Juan mountains, and they recommend taking the bus back to Durango. The round trip on the train is an exhausting 9 hours. Dubbed the Cascade Canyon Express, the winter train is a beautiful but abbreviated 5-hour trip.

Essex Steam Train—Billed as a step back in time into an unspoiled Connecticut River Valley, this 2½ hour trip includes its own riverboat cruise as part of the excursion. Reviewers are not overly impressed with the train and scenery, but they love the Becky Thatcher Riverboat with its view of river-life on the Connecticut.

Georgetown Loop Railroad—Beginning at historic Georgetown, CO (just west of Denver) this trip, which covers only a few miles and lasts one hour (round trip), proves that big things (i.e. a good time) may come in small packages. Reviewers were 90% positive and recommended the excursion, especially in the fall, and especially for families with small children.

Grand Canyon Railroad—Want to avoid the congested parking at the Grand Canyon? Then take the Grand Canyon Railroad from Williams, AZ, 64 miles to the South Rim. First class tickets get oversized seats and bar service, but the Luxury Dome option goes all out with a dome top, lounge below (bar and cocktails) and morning and afternoon snacks. The train departs daily at 9:30 a.m., arrives a couple of hours later at the South Rim, then, after more than three hours to explore the canyon, once again visitors climb aboard at 3:30 p.m., arriving in Williams at 5:45. Even though it is pricier, reviewers recommend upgrading to luxury.

Great Smoky Mountain Railroad—Departing from Bryson, NC, this 4-hour excursion travels 32 miles to Dillsboro and back. Reviews were mixed, but fans suggest that you get a good host or hostess (not sure if you can pick) and book the premium open-air gondola.

Green Mountain Scenic Railroad—Operating between Chester, VT, and the ski run at Ludlow, this antique railroad is best known for its two-hour fall foliage rides. Reviewers rave about the color, as well as the valleys and quaint towns. Also, check out the foliage dinner train.

Leadville, Colorado & Southern Railroad—Starting at Leadville, CO, you are already in the highest incorporated city in North America. The LC&S then transports you up another 1,000' for a round-trip ride of a little over two hours. Reviewers talk about the view from the top where they are surrounded by Colorado 14ers (peaks over 14,000' high).

Pikes Peak Railway—The world's highest cog railroad, in a little over one hour, will take you nine miles (straight up) to the summit of Pikes Peak. You are on the top for about 40 minutes (where you can walk around and view the gift shop and museum) and then you return to Manitou Springs (about a 3 hour trip). Reviewers are taken by the views (any seat seems to have them), and they suggest dressing warmly and booking early.

Mount Washington Cog Railway—If Pikes Peak is the world's highest cog railway, the Mount Washington Cog Railway (dating from the 1860s) is the first. The train departs at Marshfield Base station in northern New Hampshire, from where it ascends the western face of Mount Washington, a summit which boasts the coldest, windiest weather in America. Still, its passengers love the views, the informative narration by the conductor, and the pizza, soup and PB&J sandwiches on the top.

Napa Valley Wine Train—With trips from 3 hours to a full day, this train features elegant cars, gourmet cuisine and a tour of the lush vineyards of California's Napa Valley. It's both the most highly rated and expensive of American scenic railways. A full-day tour can cost $350.

New Tygart Flyer—This 4-hour, 46-mile round trip features an "S" curve tunnel, high bridge and miles of mountain views. There are assigned seats so you will want to make reservations. Reviewers extol perks in the depot town of Elkins (hotels, restaurants) and the "numerous small creeks and waterfalls" on both sides of the train.

Potomac Eagle Scenic Railroad—West Virginia has its share of scenic railroads, and the Potomac Eagle in Romney is one of the best. Offering several routes to various destinations, the Trough Trip is a tourist favorite. This 3-hour, narrated trip features a vintage dining car with gourmet entrees and excellent views of wildlife—deer, hawks and the signature bald eagle, of which there are many in the trough (a 6-mile wooded gorge on the route).

Redwood Forest Steam Train—If it's redwoods you want, it's redwoods you will get in the one-hour, round-trip from Roaring Camp, CA to the summit of Bear Mountain. Travel over trestles and through towering redwoods on the way up; then enjoy the western town of Roaring Camp. Reviewers suggest riding in the open-air carriage. Also, you can ride the train west to the beach at Santa Cruz.

Royal Gorge Route Railroad—Beginning at Cañon City, Co, the 2-hour, round-trip excursion runs along the bank of the Arkansas River 1'100' below the top of the Royal Gorge. Reviewers rate it high for a friendly staff (the train is family-owned), stunning views and better-than-average food. They suggest finding "water-side" seating. Just ask.

Stone Mountain Scenic Railroad—This 30-minute ride encircles the perimeter of Stone Mountain Park, east of Atlanta. Georgia's most visited attraction, Stone Mountain features huge depictions of confederate Civil War heroes (including their horses) etched into stone. Reviewers report enjoying the ride and suggest you view the museum and take the tram to the top of the mountain.

Tioga Central Railroad—During the tourist season (June-October), the Tioga Central operates excursion trips between Wellsboro, PA and Corning, NY. The most popular is a 24-mile roundtrip route from downtown Wellsboro to the northern end of Lake Hammond. Reviewers like the scenic lake, the fall foliage and the special dinner train.

Verde Canyon Railway—The 20-mile, 3.5-hour route follows the Verde River north from Clarkdale, AZ to the ghost town of Perkinsville and back. Each train has an observation car, bartender and guide. Guests write of a friendly staff, "nice appetizer" on board, and a grill with good sandwiches at the station. Says one passenger, "Get the upper Verde margarita!"

Wilmington and Western Railroad—Departing from Wilmington, DE, this railroad travels about 10 miles to Hockessin, where passenger can detrain and check out the shops and eateries of the destination town before returning to Wilmington (all told about a 2½ hour trip). Passengers write of beautiful scenery, excellent conditions onboard and an engaging train staff.

Alaska Railroad

It seems that, both in the American imagination and in reality, nothing compares with the beauty of the Alaskan frontier. And, as one who has ridden one, nothing gets you closer to that frontier than an Alaskan train.

The Alaska Railroad contains 470 miles of track stretching from Seward in the south to Fairbanks in the north. Some routes vary with the season. Following are your choices:

Coastal Classic—The Coastal Classic runs from Anchorage south through the Kenai Peninsula to Seward, where it sits for seven hours before returning in the evening.

Denali Star—Every day in the summer, the Denali Star departs Anchorage, passing through Wasilla, Talkeetna and Denali National Park, on a 12-hour journey to Fairbanks. A sister train does the same from Fairbanks south to Anchorage.

Glacier Discovery—This train offers daily round trips from Anchorage south to Whittier, Spencer Glacier and Grandview.

Aurora Winter—From September to mid-May, the Aurora Winter makes 12-hour weekend trips from Anchorage to Fairbanks (up on Saturday; back on Sunday).

The Rocky Mountaineer

The Rocky Mountaineer offers scenic tours through the Canadian Rockies. The key word is "tours." Each trip contains day-time train excursions with layovers in upscale hotels along the way. The line offers Silver Leaf and Gold Leaf service. Both are outfitted with plush glass-dome coaches, and both serve onboard meals, but there are perks to the Gold Leaf. Consult their website for particulars. Following are the most popular trips.

First Passage to the West—from Vancouver to Banff/Lake Louise. Features two days onboard with one night lodging in Kamloops. Passenger reviews are effusive: "The mental pictures of what we thought this trip would be were a mere fraction of how beautiful the trip actually was."

Journey through the Clouds—Vancouver to Jasper. Two days rail travel with one night in Kamloops. This route, which is accessible only by rail, features a view of Mount Robson, Canada's highest peak. Reviews praise the food, views and helpful staff. Again, passenger praise is over the top: "Truly, a trip of a lifetime."

Rainforest to Gold Rush—Vancouver to Whistler and Quesnel. Two to three days on board with two nights lodging. Passengers see hidden lakes and canyons as well as the historic Cariboo gold rush region. Reviewers are taken with the wildlife: "We saw plenty of wildlife: bears, mountain goats, deer, eagles and great blue herons."

VIA Rail Canada

VIA Rail Canada provides the only cross-country routes that allow you to sleep onboard—from Vancouver to Toronto (east-west) or Montreal to Halifax (north-south). Both trains run year round. Take a look at their trains and accommodations online (www.viarail.ca). Our neighbors to the north seem to have written the book on railroad elegance and convenience. But you do have to pay for it.

VIA also offers a variety of tours in the Canadian Rockies, which include lodging and off-train excursions. You can check them out online.

More than Trains

This chapter has been mostly about locomotives, but there are many more fun rides.

For instance, to get more fun from your automobile, choose the right vehicle for your experience. How about renting a convertible sports car to navigate a beautiful, pastoral road in, say, New Hampshire, Vermont or Kentucky?

Or choose a limousine to pick up couple friends for a night out on Valentine's. Add more fun, and make it a surprise for spouses and/or friends.

If you're in mountains, see the high country from four-wheel-only roads in a jeep or ATV. I recommend the beautiful Alpine Loop in the San Juan Range of southwest Colorado. Lake City, Silverton and Ouray all have jeep rental companies where you can either take a tour or drive yourself.

Do you want to avoid the touristy motels in town but don't want to rough it in a tent? Then consider a travel trailer or motor home. Both are available to rent as well as buy. Want to add more fun? Join friends in the experience. Just ask around on social media.

Have you always wanted to ride a Harley? Why not now? Just get some lessons and be prudent. And, if you feel unstable on two wheels, there are three-wheel versions (with the single wheel either in front or behind). Do some test rides to determine your preference.

Have you admired classic cars? Would you like to own one? Check out a local club. In addition to restoring or improving their wheels, these people enjoy tours and shows and a plethora of events related to their hobby.

And, even in the 21st century, there are still animals of transport. Have you ridden in a horse-drawn wagon, buggy or sleigh? You can. How about a dog sled? There are places. A sled pulled by reindeer? Yep. Do an online search. It's part of the fun.

Visiting the Grand Canyon? You can take a mule train to the bottom.

Want to ride a camel or elephant? There are places. Check it out.

5

Bon Appétit

It's one of life's greatest pleasures. I'm talking about food. The French have a phrase for it: "Bon appétit," which literally translates "good appetite," but, used in conversation, means "enjoy your food."

In researching the topic, my question was "what specifics could I share that will help readers do that?" I could write about ways of making meals special or give suggestions on how to slow down and really savor food, something our European friends seem to do well (lunch hours are more like two hours). But I was more interested in the kinds of foods—the specific dishes—we enjoy.

A 2021 CNN article tried to do that. "American food: The 50 greatest dishes" listed the choices the CNN travel writer thought were most favorite with Americans. The article is what academics call qualitative research. No one was surveyed. These are just the opinions of the writer.

And I agreed with most of the selections (34 of the 50 would be on my own list). But I would leave off the Twinkies, fortune cookies and beef jerky, and would add southwest favorites like tacos, tamales and rellenos.

Which is what I decided to do—make my own list. So following are dishes I enjoy most or—in some cases—hope to one day enjoy (they sound like something I should try). Maybe you'll find new items for your own menu or maybe this will motivate you to create your own list. Whatever you choose, bon appétit!

First, I have a quick caveat. Food needs to make us healthy as well as happy. Which doesn't mean you can't eat rich desserts. It just means that if you do (i. e. partake of the high sugar stuff), you'll need to balance with a lower overall calorie intake, more good carbs, plenty of protein, high fiber foods and regular exercise. I'll let you figure out what that will look like for you.

Appetizers

Nachos—These yummy treats were allegedly invented by Ignacio "Nacho" Anaya in Piedras Negras, Mexico (just across the river from Eagle Pass, TX) where the International Nacho Festival is held each October. I like them with beef (ground, shredded or fajita style). Add cheese and beans (I prefer whole to refried); then garnish with guacamole, sour cream, jalapeños and whatever else will fit on the plate.

Salsa, guacamole and chips—I could have these before any meal. Do you see an ethnic theme in my choices?

Jalapeño poppers—Bacon wrapped with cream cheese filling. Yummy.

Sliders—If I'm not having a whole burger, I'll have the cheeseburger sliders with pickle and catsup.

Fried pickles, green beans, jalapeños—Heck, bread and fry just about any veggie, and I'll try it. Good with ranch dressing.

Zucchini bites—See the above.

Buffalo wings—In 1964, Teresa Bellissimo made her city famous when she cooked her first batch of spicy wings at the Anchor Bar in Buffalo, New York. I like them as appetizers or on salads.

Deviled eggs—The deviled egg can be traced to the Andalusian region of Spain during the 13th century. The modern day version seems to show up at most of my family's holiday events, and you had better be near the front of the line if you want one.

Soups, Salads and Sandwiches

Tomato bisque—According to open.edu, the Europeans started making tomato soup in the 16th century when ships brought the plant back from South America. However, in 1897, Joseph Campbell, founder of the soup company, came up with our modern version of tomato soup. I list it because it's my wife's favorite.

Tortilla chicken soup—If you like Tex-Mex, you'll like this. Make sure to add plenty of fresh tortilla strips.

Broccoli, cheese and jalapeño soup—It's the favorite start to one of our favorite meals.

Homemade chili—I make an Atkin's friendly version with plenty of ground beef and fresh tomatoes rather than tomato sauce. There's nothing better on a cold winter's day, and you can freeze for later meals and to use on hot dogs and in Frito pie (see below).

Frito pie—Add Fritos, diced onion and shredded cheese to your chili, and you have one of America's favorite dishes. It is thought to have been invented in Texas by Daisy Doolin, the mother of the founder of the Frito Corporation.

Beef stew—Can't beat it on a cold day. My favorite has multiple pieces of pan-seared round steak and brats with plenty of veggies (corn, celery, onion and the like), salt, pepper and Italian seasoning. We make it in a slow cooker.

Green chili stew—A traditional New Mexican recipe, this dish features deliciously tender pieces of pork in a green chili base. I like fresh roasted chiles from the Chile Capital of the World, Hatch, New Mexico. You can order them (prepared and frozen) online.

Posole—A traditional Mexican stew made with pork, hominy and red chiles.

Jambalaya—Chicken, sausage, shrimp and a variety of veggies and spices served with rice. I'm pretty sure the only qualification for serving a successful pot of jambalaya is that you were born in Louisiana.

Crispy chicken salad—My favorite has shredded iceburg lettuce with fresh cherry tomatoes and shredded carrots with cut-up fried chicken strips and a honey-mustard dressing.

Grape chicken salad—A cold salad with chunk pieces of chicken breast in a mayo base with chopped celery, nuts and grapes. Good on a sandwich or by itself.

Apricot chicken salad—The above with apricots instead of grapes.

Mango chicken salad—My recipe has diced mangos with cherry tomatoes and water chestnuts served on a bed of romaine lettuce and baby spinach. Top with a honey mustard dressing.

Taco salad—Everything you put in a taco shell can go in a taco salad. I like mine with ground beef and no beans, and I like it served in one of those edible flour tortilla bowls. If you do add beans, use whole pintos or black beans.

Grilled cheese sandwich—I put a good slab of cheddar cheese between two thin slices of bread and fry with butter in a cast iron skillet. Good with slices of dill or sweet pickles.

Tuna melt—A grilled cheese sandwich with albacore tuna (mixed with mayo) added to the cheese.

Barbeque beef sandwich—Chop your smoked brisket (make sure to include some fat) into small pieces and serve on hamburger buns with barbeque sauce and sweet relish. I like the Head Country brand of the sauce.

Chicken salad sandwich—Combine boiled and diced chicken with chopped celery, parsley leaves, ground pepper, mayo and a hint of lemon juice. Be sure to toast the bread.

Meatball sub—The meatballs are the secret. Look online for a recipe that fits your taste. I like mine on a hoagie roll with marinara sauce and parmesan cheese.

Peanut butter and jelly sandwiches—I still eat them, mostly when on long hikes when I need quick energy. The peanut butter has to be extra crunchy.

BLT—Crispy bacon and fresh tomatoes are indispensable.

Breads

Sourdough, pita and Italian breads make an ordinary sandwich extraordinary.

Cornbread, hush puppies and corn pone are staples of southern cooking. I like my cornbread with chili or beans, and fish and chips go better with hushpuppies. By the way, my cornbread recipe calls for diced green chiles, cream corn, milk, eggs and grated cheddar cheese. You'll find something close to it on the back of a Martha White yellow cornbread mix.

Breakfast

Traditional American—I'm thinking of the staples: eggs (fried, scrambled or boiled), a meat (pork sausage—links or patties—bacon or ham), hash browns (crispy) and toast (wheat) or biscuit. OK, I'm hungry. My favorite place for traditional American? The Pantry in Santa Fe.

Omelets—I can feed seven using the cast iron skillet. There are so many varieties of meat and veggies. I like sausage, cheddar cheese, tomatoes and mushrooms with some peppers thrown in for a kick.

Pancakes or waffles—The store mixes work for me (Bisquick). You can add or withhold liquid (milk or water) to determine thickness. And I like to add blueberries (fresh or frozen) and pecan pieces. They're best if cooked medium high in the cast iron skillet, lightly oiled. Oh, don't forget the butter (no margarine spreads) and maple syrup. And we add peanut butter at my house.

Breakfast burritos—Mytwisters.com says the breakfast burrito was invented in New Mexico in 1975. Makes sense. Because the absolute best is found at Tia Sophia's just off the plaza in Santa Fe. Whatever you put in the burrito (and there are many choices), be sure to top it with New Mexico red sauce. Tia's also offers green sauce and Christmas (both red and green). Come early if you don't want to stand in line.

Biscuits and gravy—This is my signature dish in the Bellah family, always served on Christmas morning. It's just flour, milk, water and Jimmy Dean sausage, but I can't tell you how I make the gravy (a pinch of this here; add that; use a fork and whisk to make it smooth). Oh, you can't add too much fresh ground black pepper.

Cinnamon roll—Ask Michael's Kitchen in Taos, NM how they bake theirs. Saturated with cinnamon and topped with a light but tasty icing, this is the best.

Main Entrees

Mother's pot roast—We cook it like she did. A chuck or arm roast placed in a large pot surrounded with cut up potatoes, carrots and onion. Mom added a couple of cups of water; we supplemented that with wine and other seasonings. The oven temp? Depends. When will you get home from church?

Turkey and dressing—It must be the idea of turkey and dressing I love. I rarely eat it except on Thanksgiving. But right on schedule in early November, I start fantasizing, and by mid-month I've arranged for all the ingredients. Since we became empty nesters, we have someone else cook the bird, giblet gravy and dressing, and we concern ourselves with the complementing dishes (things like green bean casserole, jalapeño cheese grits and pecan pie). Whoops, it's not November, and I've already started to dream again.

Chicken fried steak—Lamesa and Bandera, TX both claim to have invented it, but most likely the chicken fry (as we call it here in West Texas) came to the Lone Star State via our German and Austrian immigrant farmers who created a kind of Texas Weiner schnitzel. The recipe is easy. Tenderize a thin cut of beef (maybe sirloin or round steak), dip in milk, then flour, then toss in a hot, greased skillet until golden brown. Drain and serve with white gravy (add a generous amount of ground black pepper). Why is it called chicken fried (there is no chicken in it)? Because it's prepared much like fried chicken. Serve with mashed potatoes, fried okra and/or French fries.

Meatloaf—If you like ground beef, here's another way to fix it. And if you want to lower the carbs, use diced tomatoes rather than tomato sauce for your base. Goes well with mashed potatoes and brown gravy.

Smoked brisket—I buy a trimmed brisket (8-10 lbs.); then smoke it over mesquite for three hours (indirect heat of 300-350°); then put it in the oven at 215° for 12 hours. Slice the lean end, and chop the more fatty one. This is fall-off-the-fork tender. Serve with Head Country barbecue sauce.

Spare ribs—Pork spare ribs are a pretty inexpensive meat. I smoke them similar to the brisket, but with modified times—two hours in the smoker, two hours at 275° in the oven. Yep, they will fall off the fork, too.

Burgers—I hand-pack a ½ pound patty made of 80% lean Angus beef. After seasoning liberally with salt and pepper, cook over hot mesquite coals (no flame) for approximately four minutes on each side (for medium well burgers).

Brats—I put these on the grill immediately after removing the burgers. I like the fully cooked product we get from a German American family in the

Texas hill country. The mesquite fire not only warms but gives a taste of smoke and searing. We use them mostly for hot dogs, although the wife chops them for a pasta salad, and I've been known to eat them with sauerkraut.

Cheeseburger—Did you know there is a National Cheeseburger Day? And did you know the entrée was an American invention? That honor is claimed by both California and Kentucky, but the Humpty Dumpty Drive-In in Denver, CO has both a court order and a trademark certifying their bragging rights.

Green chili burger—The Owl Bar and Café in San Antonio, NM claims to have invented the green chili burger where the recipe has not changed since 1948. Makes sense to me—San Antonio is less than 100 miles north of Hatch, home of the most famous New Mexico chiles.

Hot dog—Supposedly, a German immigrant named Charles Feltman invented the hot dog when he placed a German sausage (a "frank" or "frankfurter") on a bun to avoid getting a plate dirty. Yet, making the treat popular was left to New York City's Coney Island whose name is now synonymous with the food. I like mine with chili, cheese, mustard and onion.

Corn dog—Place a frankfurter in a cornmeal batter and deep fry and you have a corn dog. And no trip to a county or state fair is complete without eating one.

Grilled steaks—The greatest challenge to any outdoor griller is getting a steak right. I say choosing the right cut is paramount. Make sure you have good marbling (white flecks and streaks of fat). Next season the meat well with a rub or salt and pepper (it's almost impossible to put on too much); then cook over hot coals two minutes to a side (should leave a good sear mark—black lines). Finish with indirect heat in a smoker or oven until you test with a meat thermometer to get the right doneness.

Fajitas—The fajita is a more modern invention (some say 1969) made popular when rodeo chefs grilled skirt steak ("faja" in Spanish) and placed it, alongside veggies in a tortilla. I grill both beef and chicken fajita meat (the chicken does better in a Pellet grill). Next we spread these, alongside warmed tortillas, on a table filled with many condiments (peppers, grilled onions, guacamole, sour cream, shredded cheese). Then diners build their own fajitas to suit.

Tacos—It seems tacos were first made by Mexican silver miners in the 1700s. Mexican migrants introduced them to America in the early 1900s, but it was Glen Bell, the founder of Taco Bell who, starting in the early '60s, made them popular in the U.S. Today over 40 million Americans eat at Taco Bell every week. I say choose your taco by the taco meat. Find the meat you like, and you've found your taco of choice.

Enchiladas—Enchiladas also were invented in Mexico, but much earlier, in the time of the Aztecs. I have two favorites. The first is taco meat wrapped in a blue corn tortilla and covered with New Mexico red sauce. The second, melted cheese wrapped in a flour tortilla and covered with tomatillo sauce (a green sauce that tastes like a tart tomato).

Tamales—Tamales also date from the days of the Aztecs. A tamale is made with corn dough called masa, filled with meat (pork or beef) and steamed in a corn husk. I like mine covered with hatch queso sauce.

Pasta

Pizza—Forty percent of Americans eat pizza once a week, and I'm not one of them. I like it OK. It's just too many carbs for me to manage with all the other things I like to eat. However . . .

Chicago style pizza—If I lived in Chicago, I'd be in trouble. For from the first time I tried Chicago-style pizza (in the windy city itself), I was addicted. What can I say? That deep dish of meat, cheese (and a whole lot of other tasty stuff) set in a thick scrumptious crust was too much to resist. So I got out of town. Fast. And I'm not going back. An addict knows when the temptation is too great.

Fish

Fish and chips—Because the dish is rich in both fat and carbs, I eat it sparingly. The best I've had was in a pub in London.

Wild Alaskan Salmon—We once had salmon at a little outdoor stand in Talkeetna, Alaska. They cook it like I cook burgers, over real wood coals. I remember telling friends it was the best I've tasted. Now, I know why. Not only was it fresh (as opposed to canned); over 90% of U.S. salmon is raised on fish farms. The Alaska variety comes from the ocean where the fish make those seasonal runs up inland waterways to spawn and die. Don't know why, but it makes them taste better.

Catfish—It's the staple fish of our area of West Texas. I like it fried, but the blackened variety is still tasty and much better for me.

Jumbo shrimp—What can I say? Who doesn't enjoy shrimp, except those like my wife who have allergies to shell fish. I like them boiled and chilled with cocktail sauce, and fried and served with hushpuppies and fries. Again, the fried variety has too many carbs to eat frequently.

Lobster rolls and Maryland crab cakes—I've had neither of these, but they are on my bucket list. Can't say why. They just sound sumptuous.

Sides

French fries—we get ours extra, extra crispy.

Potato chips—Many restaurants now make their own, which is an improvement over the store-bought variety. Except for the new "kettle cooked" spuds, which I like regardless of where I find them.

Hash browns and country potatoes—A great addition to the traditional American breakfast.

Baked potatoes—I love them loaded, but, again, am eating them infrequently because of the carbs.

Corn on the cob—Same as above. But if I must, I'll smother it with butter and ground black pepper.

Green beans—Low in carbs and tasty. I flavor with bacon bits.

Broccoli and cheese—In addition to making a good soup, add rice and it's one of my favorite casseroles. Put in jalapeños for a kick.

Squash—I like it baked in a casserole with eggs, milk, nutmeg, crackers and cheddar cheese.

Desserts

It seems that American desserts consist mainly of pies and cakes so that's where I'll start.

Pies or cobblers

Did you know there is a National Pie Day? Yep, January 23. And did you know that, according to the American Pie Council, 59% of Americans "consider pie an appropriate late-night snack," and 20% of us "have eaten an entire pie?" Scary, huh?

Well, I won't confess to the entire pie thing, but I'm pretty sure I've partaken in the late night hours. So since the Pie Council says six in ten of you share my addiction, here are my favorites that you may enjoy, too:

Apple—Yes, it's true. Apple is America's favorite. Fruit pies were first made in Europe during the 1500s and came to America with the colonists (along with seeds to grow the trees—there are no fruit trees native to the U.S.).

Banana cream—The bananas need to be right, not too green, not overly ripe.

Blackberry—I wish we could get these fresh in my part of America, but frozen blackberries are still flavorful.

Blueberry—See the above. Michigan, Maine and Oregon produce the most blueberries.

Cherry—Though they grow best in the northern states, I'm pretty sure there are cherry trees in most states. English tradition says Queen Elizabeth I made the first cherry pie in the UK. Cherry is my favorite cobbler (with the perfunctory scoop of ice cream on top).

Chocolate cream—Evidently, the "cream" designation refers to the rich custard or pudding in these pies. I say every pie so designated is a keeper.

Chocolate meringue—Cooks tell me that meringue is a whipped mixture of egg whites and sugar. Sounds simple, but from observing the finished product, I think it's pretty difficult to make all those swirls appear uniform and slightly brown.

Coconut cream—Because of the difficulty creating the technology to shred and dry coconuts, this pie didn't make it into the American mainstream until the early 1900s. Today, it's my favorite.

Key lime—This treat is so named for the small, pungent lime grown in the Florida Keys. All I can say is Floridians should be proud.

Lemon meringue—I like tart (as opposed to overly sweet) desserts, and this is one of the best.

Peach—Fresh peaches (even good frozen peaches) are hard to find. We buy ours from Cunningham Orchards in Palisade, CO. Big trucks make their way through our part of Texas every August. We buy several boxes, wash and slice the fruit, and freeze in quart bags. The cobblers are to-die-for throughout the year.

Pecan—The biggest discussion surrounding this dessert is pronunciation. Is it pee-can ("a" as in "pan") or pee-caun ("a" as in "father")? In my world, it is the second. It seems that pecan pie entered the American mainstream in the 1920s when Karo syrup started putting the recipe on its bottles. Anyway, I have to have a piece at Christmas dinner.

Pumpkin—I can't finish the Thanksgiving meal without a piece topped with whipped cream or vanilla ice cream.

Strawberry rhubarb—I don't like rhubarb by itself, but when you add it to a strawberry pie, something magical happens.

Cakes

I'm not as much a fan of cakes as I am of pies, but the following will get my attention:

Chocolate—This one is to cakes what apple is to pies. Evidently, chocolate cake is not only America's favorite but the world's favorite as well.

German Chocolate—The name comes, not from a nation or ethnic group, but from Sam German, an Englishman who invented a baking chocolate for Baker's Chocolate Company in 1852. However, the modern day recipe did not become famous until 1957 when a Texas cook published it in a Dallas newspaper.

Carrot—Yes, the cake has real carrots in the batter, mixed with nuts like pecans or walnuts and spices like cinnamon and ginger. I say the cream cheese frosting sells it.

Red Velvet—I love the color and the taste.

Lemon—This one serves as the cake of choice for our kids' birthdays. It's a nice combination of sweet and sour.

Chocolate Peanut Butter—Actually, I have not tasted this one, but the name has captured me. Anything that combines chocolate with peanut butter has my attention.

New York cheesecake—My sources say a New York cheesecake has more cream cheese, a few extra egg yolks and additional cream than its less indulgent cousin. According to New Yorkers, the great cheesecake makers all come from the Empire State.

And Other Treats

Banana pudding—We can't have a family reunion without it. The trick is the bananas—not too green, not too ripe.

Chocolate chip cookies—You can't have too many chips. By the way, don't overcook. The dough should be done but still soft.

S'mores—These are the staple of a successful campfire get-togethers. Place two roasted marshmallows on top of a Hershey chocolate bar between two graham cracker squares, and you have a s'more (as in "I'll have some more").

Ice cream—Some say ice cream is America's favorite dessert. I say it's at least our favorite dessert side. Everything is better à la mode.

Chocolate sundae—According to thedairyalliance.com, "A pharmacist named Charles Sonntag created the treat, naming it the 'sonntag' after himself. Sonntag means Sunday in German, and so the name was translated to Sunday, and later spelled as 'sundae.'"

Banana split—The origin of this American favorite is disputed, either somewhere in Ohio (1907) or Pennsylvania (1904). But one thing is beyond questioning for this lover of the dish. The best banana split in modern times can be enjoyed at the San Juan Soda Fountain in Lake City, CO. Warning: Don't share with a 12-year-old grandchild. You'll consume only a third of the dessert.

And now . . .

I don't know about you, but I've gained 10 pounds just writing this section. So let's do something about it and move quickly to the next chapter, "Shake Your Booty."

6

Shake Your Booty

"**F**itness cuts your risk of dying; it doesn't get much more bottom line than that," wrote Drs. John Rowe and Robert Kahn in *Successful Aging: The Surprising Results of the MacArthur Foundation Study—the Most Extensive, Comprehensive Study on Aging in America*. And, in case you're envisioning push-ups, sit-ups and laps around a track, think again. Exercise can be fun. Following are some ideas:

Walking/Hiking

In 1955, at the age of 67, Grandma Emma Gatewood became the first solo female to complete the 2,168-mile Appalachian Trail. She would do it two more times before her death nearly 20 years later. You may not be interested in conquering the AT like Gatewood, but how about these?

Walk to the highest point in states near you. Most are not terribly high. Try, for instance, Guadalupe Peak in Texas (8,751'), Black Mesa in Oklahoma (4,973') or Magazine Mountain in Arkansas (2,753').

Discover walking paths in city and state parks near you. Google can help and so can Facebook. Just ask for suggestions. Make a list of at least five, and when the weather cooperates, take the journey. Be sure to carry a map and plenty of water.

Come up with a regular walking route in your own town or city. Find something that highlights the kind of views and memories that inspire you.

One day, instead of taking your routine walk, let the walk take you. Turn down less familiar streets and see new sights. It's easy to do in a small town, but I guess you need to consider safety more in large cities. But if you live in a metropolis, I suppose you could still travel to a small town and "let the walk take you." Just keep your smart phone handy to find the way back.

Make walking part of your out-of-town travel, even if it's just extended walks for shopping (still another fun thing to do).

Consider Nordic Walking. You'll need special poles for this, and you'll need to look at a video on YouTube to get the proper technique. In addition to leg muscles, this exercise tones your arms and abdomen. And while Nordic walking helps greatly on slopes, it can be done on flat terrain as well.

In addition to mountains, try hiking a canyon. In the Texas Panhandle, that would be Palo Duro Canyon, the second largest in the U.S. Also, you just can't get the good out of the Grand Canyon without hiking some of its trails. I recommend day hikes on the Bright Angel and South Kaibab. Be sure to following the Park's safety measures.

Speaking of the Grand Canyon, some of you might want to attempt some more extreme hikes. I like Mt. Elbert in Colorado (at 14,440', the second highest in the lower 48) and Wheeler in New Mexico (13,161'). Also, you can do a rim to rim in the Grand Canyon, either down and up the south rim, or a more strenuous hike from the north rim to the south. It's prudent to take more than one day and spend the night at Phantom Ranch on the canyon floor. Get on the Grand Canyon website to make plans.

If you are in the right climate for this, try snow-shoeing. Advocates of this activity point to the beauty of winter landscapes and the serenity of solitude and quietness that usually accompany this adventure. Look online to get the right equipment; you'll need lessons to get started.

Cycling

If you are a road bike enthusiast, search your area for favorite highway routes. The best will have minimal car traffic and include stopping places for rest and/or food. So take that trip. And you'll have more fun if you take friends with you.

Mountain bikes probably make more sense for us boomers. The straight handle bars are easier on the back and the larger (fat) tires make falling less likely. I recommend leaving the single track trails to younger people (whose bones heal more readily) and choose a Rails to Trails route. These are old railroad beds that have been turned into biking and hiking paths. Search the Internet for one near you (there are dozens nationwide). If you come to the Texas Panhandle, check out the Caprock Canyon Trailway near Quitaque (sounds like Kitty Quay). I recommend riding the 20-mile loop from Monk's Crossing to the top of the Caprock and back.

Go to railstotrails.org and discover the wide variety of special rides in the U.S. Choose five of these to put on your wish list. I'm looking at the George S. Mickelson Trail in the Black Hills of South Dakota. You can spread out this 108-mile ride into several days. Check out mickelsontrail.com, and you'll find outfitters who will supply all you need, including transportation to and from the trail on successive days of your trip.

Swimming/snorkeling/paddle boarding

Swimming is supposed to be the most complete exercise (involves all the major muscles). Visit your local pool or (more fun) find a lake or river with a good beach.

Speaking of beaches, if you find one at an ocean resort, they will probably offer to take you snorkeling, which is both great exercise and a lot of fun.

According to one source, over 20 million Americans participate in standup paddle boarding. Paddle boards look like surf boards, although many of them are not made of hard material but are flexible and inflatable (easier to store and transport). People who like this activity talk about the zen of gliding across a calm lake. Also, the activity works your arms and torso, and helps with balance.

Contrary to the stereotype, water aerobics is not only for the old. It provides both aerobic exercise (works your heart and lungs), and also is a form of resistance training (helps all the major muscles). And, if you talk to the people I interviewed, with the right instructor and a group of good friends, it is a lot of fun.

Shaking your booty

Since ancient times and in all cultures, dancing has been a favorite form of exercise and fun. I recommend taking a lesson if you need one (you can get these online) and—with or without a partner—try the following:

Pull up some big band music on YouTube, Spotify or Pandora, and try ballroom dancing. For elegance and romance, try a waltz or foxtrot. Or change the music to something more lively (and sexy) and learn the Cha-Cha, Tango and Rumba.

Country western dancing is in vogue in our part of the world. Put on your cowboy hat, jeans and boots and learn the two-step. You'll pick it up fast (quick step, quick step, long, long, slight pause). Then, there's the country waltz step (basically the same as ballroom but to a different vibe).

Before you're through, you'll want to learn western swing (steps are much like the jitterbug moves you saw on American Bandstand with Dick Clark) and line dancing (I'm dating myself, but I recommend the Electric Slide and the Cotton-eyed Joe).

Pull it up online and learn some Folk Dances. Try a Polka and then a Scottish. I still remember a polka step learned in Mrs. Jones's 5th grade class called the "Salty Dog Rag."

Square dancing isn't as square as you might think. You'll need to join a group for this. Look online for a local company. By the way, you need to dress for this (look it up).

If you want to step it up a bit, there are aerobic exercises set to music. Try finding a Jazzercise class, or if you're really gung ho, join a Zumba group.

Finally, you might want to visit the dances of your youth. For me that would be the rockabilly songs of the late '50s and early '60s where we "bopped" to Buddy Holly, Jerry Lee Lewis and Elvis. And with the British invasion, we dropped our partner's arm and did the more individual steps (the foot pattern is much the same as bopping and swing). So bring up one of your favorites and get lost in the '50s tonight.

Spinning at the gym

Visiting a gym is good for you, even if it seems more like work. To make it more fun, I suggest getting a personal trainer and/or a training buddy (good conversation and maybe some competition). Also, you'll find it fun to join some of the group classes like yoga or spinning (look it up; I started spinning in my 60s and love it).

7

Fun Retirement Gigs

The statistics are out. Most baby boomers cannot retire with the same cash flow as they had in their career jobs. But, not to worry—there are plenty of opportunities to work and have fun. Here are some of them:

Airbnb host—Rent out one room or your entire house to guests. For the investment (cost of remodeling or decorating), probably this business provides more return than any other.

Appraiser—Evidently, if you know or can find out how much things cost, folks (mostly bankers making loans) will pay for your knowledge. Appraisers come in all flavors (Real Estate, machinery, livestock, antiques, automobiles). Some require a degree. Most don't.

Assistant—People pay good money for assistants. There are executive assistants (help busy executives with things for which they don't have the time or desire to do themselves), personal assistants (help people of means with everything from grocery shopping to scheduling appointments to transporting family members) and virtual assistants (who do many of the things listed above from home (using a phone and computer).

Baker—Open your own bakery, and, no, you don't have to rent retail property. Cook at home and sell online, using social media to find customers. You'll probably need a city license.

Blogger—Create your own blog (find a topic on which you are an authority/or can be with study). Also, you can blog for other people. You'll make your money with advertisements (the first choice) or agreed upon payments (the second).

Bookstore owner—Are you good at finding gently used books in your community? Sell them online at your own virtual book store (take a look at the Amazon Associates Program).

Brewmaster—Yes, you can make beer for a living. Check it out online.

Bus driver—Drive charter buses on tours to interesting places. Or become a city bus driver in a picturesque place (the Grand Canyon is hiring). You'll need a CDL for this.

Business—Start your own small business. Here are some ideas: handyman (I'm always looking for one), sewing and alterations (again, in high demand), house flipper (will need some cash and a line of credit, but can be quite lucrative), printer of on-demand T-shirts, online dating consultant (seriously, look it up), videographer, travel planner (a scaled down version of the travel agent), event planner, consignment shop (you can either own or become a seller), moving company (lots of demand here and you don't have to do the heavy lifting yourself), professional organizer/declutterer (call me when you get that going), craft seller (some of the things you made in chapter 10) and online store (you can use drop shipping, which means a third party stores and ships your merchandise for you).

Car—Use your own car to transport customers (Uber and Lyft) or food (Door Dash, Uber Eats). It's called "ride sharing," and in the right locale, you can make good money. Also, you can rent your car to others (check out turo.com). Or you can drive for dealerships who need to deliver cars all over the U.S. The money is decent, and you get to drive some incredible vehicles.

Card shark—Yes, you can become a professional poker, even bridge player. The job requires knowledge, not degrees. Hint: you'd better be good at it or you'll lose your 401K.

Chocolatier—A chocolatier is a chef who specializes in making chocolate. Hey, someone has to do it.

Life coach—Do you like to mentor people? Maybe help them with the transition to retirement? Look up "life coaching" online. There are a number of training programs.

Consultant—Do you have specialized knowledge and skill from your career? Someone will pay for that. You just need to find him or her.

Cruise ship employee—Cruise lines hire food service workers, nurses, doctors, speakers, instructors (can you learn the history of various ports and present it in an interesting way?), deck hands and photographers. And the perks are obvious.

Dogs—If you like hanging out with man's (or woman's) best friend, you'll find online postings for dog sitters, dog groomers and dog trainers. I even found ones for dog psychologists and acupuncturists. I assume you will need degrees for the latter.

Drone pilot—For commercial work, it takes a degree, but how fun!

Ebay seller—According to nichepursuits.com, the following items are easy to sell on Ebay: gently used lego sets, vintage clothing(we're talking old—over 100 years), antiques, women's dresses, video games (think Madden football) and baby things (strollers, bouncers, swings and such). To figure out the business end of this (pricing, profit margins, etc.), check out resellingrevealed.com.

Events planner—Organize a variety of social and business events like conferences and conventions.

Fashion consultant—These folks use fashion and clothing styles to help people develop a more attractive and professional image. By the way, if you bite on this one, I could use your services.

Food critic—Do you like to eat at new places, and can you write interesting evaluations of your experience? Yes, people pay for this.

Food stylist—According to lifehack.org, food stylists turn food into a "piece of art," and make good money doing it.

Food truck owner—Would you like to own a restaurant but with shorter hours and fewer employees? Food trucks operate in most cities, as well as at county and state fairs.

Guide—I found online listings for hunting guides, fishing guides, rafting guides, tour guides (how about leading a ghost tour in New Orleans?), mountain trail guides and canoe trip guides. Yes, these are not for the faint of heart. Check out "Guide Jobs and Trip Leaders" at coolworks.com.

Home decorator—One website promises a certificate as a professional interior decorator with online classes lasting only six weeks. Before enrolling in this one, I'd look at local license requirements, but I'm pretty sure a community college could provide the same training with reasonable expense and time.

Home staging—If you're good at making an ordinary home look extraordinary, this is the job for you. I don't think it requires a degree, and it seems to pay well.

House sitter—Just make sure the house has good security, a full fridge and good cable. And it doesn't hurt if the location is in an attractive tourist area.

Ice cream taster—Seems as though this one requires a degree in food science, but, hey, what a gig!

Instructor—There are a plethora of jobs available for instructors, including dance, yoga, jazzercise, spinning, gun safety and use, painting (watercolor-acrylic-oil-chalk-pencil) sculpting and many more).

Personal trainer/fitness coach—It takes some formal training and a certificate, but great way to make money and stay in shape.

Peace Corps worker—There is no age limitation. I checked.

Private investigator—Fulfill your sleuth fantasies and become a private investigator. Although a background in law enforcement is useful, my sources say no special degree is needed.

Missionary—Many faith based organizations have employment opportunities for retirees. The jobs are short on salary but long on fulfillment and purpose.

National park employee—The National Park Service hires thousands of seasonal employees, and many of them are retired. What do they do? Everything from giving talks about history and nature to working at entry gates. Oh, and the jobs usually come with free housing (cabins, dorms or RV spots). I pulled up Glacier National Park for this summer, and they're advertising for wait staff, maintenance workers, customer service and hospitality. The site says you can work in a gift shop, restaurant, hotel or as a guide. So how fun is that!

Seller—In addition to those listed under Ebay, retirees have made good money selling Real Estate (will take a license), cars (new and used), RV's and more.

Shopper—Want to get paid for your favorite pastime? Personal shoppers get paid by clients who don't have the time or expertise to do their own. A mystery shopper works for a company who wants to know how good their online store is doing with customer satisfaction. According to jobmonkey.com, personal shoppers can make up to $100k while mystery shoppers max out at $70k.

Sommelier—According to lifecheck.org, a sommelier tastes wines and recommends them for a living. The salary is listed as $40-150k annually. Not a bad gig, huh?

Teacher—Pull up a college catalogue, and you will see just how many subjects one can teach (it's in the 100s). And, probably, you'll find something on the list you would enjoy teaching. Plus, you don't have to possess a degree for some classes. Leisure study programs at community colleges and lifelong learning institutes (like the OLLI in chapter eight) want knowledgeable and interesting teachers, with or without formal degrees.

Tutors—During the pandemic, some public schools paid $2,000 per week to people (many without teaching certificates) to tutor their students. In addition, there was high demand (and unusually high salaries) for substitute teachers.

Voice actor—A voice actor does voice-overs for commercials and animated cartoons. In addition, he or she narrates audio books. A good one can make $500 per hour for finished recordings.

Wedding coordinator—A wedding coordinator makes sure the wedding (and events surrounding the wedding) goes according to plan. It's a high pressure job but pays accordingly.

Writer—There are many kinds of free-lance writers, including resume writers, crossword puzzle writers and fortune cookie writers (no kidding).

YouTube channel owner/producer/star—Want to be a TV star (well, sort of)? Create your own YouTube channel (like blogging, you'll need specific content to attract viewers). You'll find many how-to videos to get you started. Once up and running,

you can make money with commercials and pro-
motion of things you have to sell.

8

The Fun of Learning

Some educators argue that trying to make learning fun dilutes it, as if academic rigor and enjoyment can't coexist. I argue the opposite. Learning not only *can be*—*it is*—fun, and in these pages I've assembled 75 things to do that will bring both pleasure and knowledge.

And, as a bonus, often that knowledge leads to even more fun. Excited? You should be.

State colleges and universities

State colleges and universities in all 50 states offer some kind of discounted tuition for seniors.

So check out the offerings in your state. Here are some examples:

Want to study geography? The University of North Dakota offers a class in World Geography, which is both online and self-paced.

Want to know the geography of your state? Texas A&M University offers GEOG 305, a study of Texas geography. Michigan State has an online Introduction to the Lakes class. And the University of New Mexico offers GEOG 445, a study of the geography of New Mexico and the Southwest.

Lifelong learning

There are 100s of colleges and universities that offer lifelong learning classes, especially designed for older students. The most popular is a consortium of 124 schools under the umbrella of the Osher Lifelong Learning Institute (OLLI). These are college-level but non-credit classes with no homework or grades (Yea!).

Google the National Resource Center for OLLI at Northwestern University. Search their Institute Directory. Click on a city near you (not necessary if you want an online class) and check out the offerings. You will be blown away. Following are recommendations:

Visit the website of the OLLI at Florida Atlantic University Boca Raton and sign up for "Does Hamilton Get Hamilton Right?" and "When We Were Apollo." For just $10 per month, you can take as many as you want of these courses.

Next check out the Texas Tech OLLI and their Fredericksburg campus. Sign up for the Zoom classes "Civil War in the Southwest" and "Spacecraft Voyages to the Moon and Other Planets" (the second is taught by a retired Navy vet who did research at NASA).

Or visit the OLLI in Prescott, AZ for a look at the films of Humphrey Bogart. Or the OLLI at Albertus Magnus College in New Haven where you can learn to raise backyard chickens or "rediscover" the world of fairy stories.

In addition, you can visit the Western Colorado OLLI at Grand Junction where you can study astronomy, watercolor or beekeeping.

After that you'll be ready for the OLLI at Boise State, which offers dozens of lectures. I recommend "The Nine Lives of Benjamin Franklin" and "Sea Otters on the Oregon Coast." Most of the OLLIs will let you take all the classes you want for a yearly membership fee (at Boise State, it is $70).

Similarly, you can attend the University of Georgia OLLI at Athens, which offers close to 100 classes on subjects from plants to the paranormal.

Or how about visiting the OLLI at the University of Nebraska, Lincoln where you can watch online testimonials from students who took the birding class and the "Introduction to Kayaking"? Do this, then enroll in the classes yourself.

Or you can visit neighboring Ames, IA where the Iowa State OLLI offers "American Writers of the Lost Generation," "Museums around the World: From Ames to Australia" and "Finding Our Song: Learning to Play the Native American Flute."

Finally, you might want to travel to the northeast extremity of the U.S. to the OLLI in Bar Harbor, ME, which offers classes on "Winter Birds and the Transition to Spring." Or avoid the drive and take their Zoom class "Introduction to Nature Writing," which includes virtual trips to Acadia National Park.

The Great Courses (now Wondrium)

After I discovered this website (wondrium.com), I dropped out of sight for three weeks while I sampled the courses. For only $20 per month ($15 if you pay quarterly), you can watch and listen to world renown professors deliver 30-minute lectures on the topic of your choice.

I recommend "The Irish Identity" taught by Dr. Marc C. Connor. It's a course that blends great Irish literature with the nation's history and culture. If you want to know more about Great Britain, try "Great Tours: England, Scotland and Wales" taught by Emory University's Patrick N. Allitt. I ended up watching all 36 lectures. If you want more ancient history, try "The Greek World" or "Ancient Rome."

If you're into military history, there's "Unsung Heroes of World War II in Europe," or for the other part of that war, "World War II, the Pacific Theater." Or you can go further back with "The American Civil War" or "The Pirate Wars of 1718."

For a more multicultural experience, check out "The Mongul Empire," "The Ottoman Empire" or "Understanding Imperial China."

Classical music lovers can choose from whole classes on Bach, Mozart, Hayden, Beethoven, Brahms and others. If you want a more recent genre, you can study "Great Music of the 20th Century" or more specifically, "England, the 1960s and the Triumph of the Beatles."

For art lovers, there's "Artists of the Italian Renaissance," a course on the Louvre where students are treated to a virtual tour of the Louvre's collection of famous masterpieces, and "The World's Greatest Churches," a look at the fascinating architecture of the world's great cathedrals.

TED Talks

TED (originally, an acronym for Technology, Entertainment and Design) is a nonprofit organization begun in 1984 with the purpose of sharing life-and-world-changing ideas through short, powerful talks (the average is 18 minutes). Today (in more than 100 languages) they touch on a variety of subjects from science to business to ethics.

Go to their website (www.ted.com) and check out their 25 most popular talks. I recommend the following:

"Do schools kill creativity" with Sir Ken Robinson offers good advice for both grandkids and their grandparents. Sometimes creativity means not doing what everyone expects of us.

In "Your body language may shape who you are," Amy Cuddy shows how we can shape how we think and act by shaping how we stand or sit.

Simon Sinek explains the success of Steve Jobs and Martin Luther King Junior with three circles. His main point is the same as mine in The Best Is

Yet To Be. It's the "why" behind what we do that counts, even more than the "what" and "how."

Robert Waldinger, also featured in the above mentioned book, answers the question—"What makes a good life." His lessons from the longest study on happiness should be required listening for all retirees.

She is not in the top 25 talks, but spoken-word-poet Sara Kay has two pieces that are both entertaining and uplifting. Check out "How many lives can you live?" and "If I should have a daughter."

Community colleges

Finally, your local community college has an abundance of continuing education or leisure study classes. Pick up a catalogue and enjoy.

9

The Sound of Music

According to statista.com, Americans spend around 27 hours per week listening to music. Spotify adds that there are over 1,300 music genres in the world, including Norwegian Hip Hop, Swedish Reggae and Spanish Punk. There's also Black Sludge, Math Rock, Vaporwave and No Wave.

Music is one of those universal pleasures that people of all cultures and ages enjoy. For retirees, I suggest the following:

Attend a concert. Go as a group, and it will be more fun.

I searched for performers liked by baby boom audiences and found the following who are returning to the road after the 2020 shutdown: The Rolling Stones, Eagles, Lynyrd Skynyrd, Elton John, Billy Joel, Hall and Oates, Chicago, Earth, Wind & Fire, Jimmy Buffett, Rod Stewart, Eric Clapton, ZZ Top, Metallica, James Taylor and Bruce Springsteen. You can find more names at cheapism.com.

Choose another search term (country music, pop, Las Vegas or Branson performers) and make your own list of an event or events you want to attend.

Attend a music festival. In Texas we have the South by Southwest Festival in Austin and the Kerrville Folk Festival (which, by the way, is the longest running music festival in North America).

Did you know you can attend concerts at sea? Concerts at Sea Rock and Roll Cruises offer a 7-day Caribbean cruise onboard the Sky Princess with nightly entertainment furnished by the likes of Gary Puckett of the Union Gap, Paul Revere's Raiders, The Vogues and Peter Rivera, once lead singer of Rare Earth. Check out their upcoming trips online.

Plan a trip to your city or regional symphony, master chorale, university band concert, ballet or opera. Stretch yourself. You might discover a new love.

Attend a Broadway musical—on Broadway if you can afford it. If not, high schools and universities have some talented young stars.

Do a home Internet concert. Find your own favorite music or musician and enjoy. I like a playlist with Dolly Parton and Kenny Rogers.

Become a groupie for a band or artist. Seriously. Every town has garage bands that can be fun to follow. Just for the record, I am a "Prairie Dogs" groupie.

Learn to play a new instrument. Try the guitar, harmonica or piano. You can find lessons on the Internet.

By the way, they have camps to learn or improve technique on instruments (search the Internet for "harmonica camps").

Join a choir.

Take a voice lesson.

Pull out the old band instrument from high school. For me that would be a sousaphone—not sure Charlotte will let one live here.

Host or attend a house concert featuring a less famous band. Less famous does not mean less enjoyable.

Watch a high school or college marching band.

Plan a musical trip or tour, maybe listening to jazz in Memphis and New Orleans.

Become a Karaoke singer (you sing a popular song accompanied by a recorded band and watched by other Karaoke fans). Search "Karaoke Bars Near Me."

Go caroling with friends at Christmas. Yes, they still do this. Ask friends on social media.

10

The Fun of Making Things

At age 65, three years after leaving office, President George W. Bush decided he needed a new challenge and that he wanted to learn to paint. A friend introduced him to Dallas-based artist Gail Norfleet who would go on to meet with the aspiring artist for three hours every Monday afternoon for two years. Later, Norfleet would comment, "He wasn't the most gifted student I ever taught, but he was the most persistent."

The result? In 2014 Bush's portraits of 24 of the world's leaders went on display in the George W. Bush Presidential Library in Dallas. Even skeptical art critics admitted this novice had "a way with paint." Bush's next project showcased his admiration for veterans as he assembled 90 sketches of post 9-11 service men and women.

Bush's latest work is a collection of 43 immigrants, which in 2021 appeared as both an exhibit and a book: *Out of Many, One: Portraits of American Immigrants*.

Painting

I can't promise you will get your own exhibit (it helps to be a former president), but following are some ideas for pursuing the art of painting, an activity I'm pretty sure will also bring a smile to your retiree face.

Find a teacher and/or class—You may not be able to afford private lessons, but there are a variety of online and face-to-face classes from which to choose. Take some time to search and read the reviews. Also, many teachers recommend group classes because of student interaction. It seems that viewing and commenting on the work of others helps your own.

Decide what you want to paint. Teachers say that you need to care about your subject matter. And, supposedly, the more you care, the better you will paint. Some advise touring art galleries and finding out what captivates you. Others say to tour your own, everyday world with a view to discovering what is pleasing that you might want to paint.

Also, you need to choose the medium. What substance will you put on the page or canvas, things like acrylics, oils or watercolors? One teacher suggests you start with color pencils, which are relatively inexpensive and easy to use. He urged getting the best. The best materials may not guarantee success, but inferior ones certainly can lead to an inferior result.

George Bush learned something of art history and fundamentals, something you will find in your class and that you might augment with a good book. Do some searching.

Bush asked his teacher how he could improve. Her answer: "Keep painting," which I'm sure led to better results and more fun for our 43rd president.

Finally, my suggestion as a writing teacher is that, once you have revised and improved your work, share it with others. Just as writers write to be read, I'm pretty sure painters paint so others can see.

Knitting

Knitting is a fiber art. Instead of oil or lead, your medium is some type of yarn or thread. An activity enjoyed by all ages, knitting seems to be especially popular with retirees. Where do you start?

My knitting friends say you first find other knitters—maybe by going to a fiber arts store in your town or region. I suppose other knitters help you explore various projects and techniques, but judging by my interviews, it has a lot to do with camaraderie. Knitters knit while they hang out and do life together—still another fun thing to do in retirement.

What will you knit?

It seems that beginners start with hats, scarves, shawls (which, seems to me, are just larger scarves), ponchos, bags, baby booties, pillow covers and coasters. I still have a long, winter cap (think of a Santa hat with an extra long tail) that my grandmother knitted for me in 1963.

More experienced knitters can make, well, almost anything. Feltmagnet.com lists knit items that sell well at craft fairs, things like children's mittens and hats (with the facsimile of a favorite animated movie character sewn on), headbands, boot cuffs (look it up), potato chip scarves (they look like their namesake), kitchen dishcloths, towels, placemats and toys (see them online; I'm taken by knitted bunny rabbits, elephants and dolls).

Needlepoint

Needlepoint, I am told, is a type of canvas work where threads are stitched on a canvas to create a picture or design. According to needlepoint-for-fun.com, this technique can be used to make an inset pillow, or pin cushion or ornament. Or you can personalize a hand bag. In addition, needlepoint canvases (featuring a series of scenes or designs) can be framed and displayed on a wall "gallery-style."

Also, you can sew many needlepoint pieces together to make a patchwork that could cover a pillow or even a sofa. I like the online pictures of Christmas stockings decorated with needlepoint.

Quilting

My family is blessed with an abundance of quilts that have been passed from one generation to the next, which, one quilting website tells me, is the reason for making them—to preserve one's history. Perhaps, that's what a friend of mine has in mind when she sews together old T-shirts into a memorial quilt she gives to parents whose children have passed.

But quilts also celebrate the present. One source says they reflect the "passion and love a quilter has for life itself."

Not being a quilter, I can't verify the motives of the makers, but what I can say with some certainty is that quilting, like knitting, seems to be a team sport. I found online quilt study groups, quilt guilds, quilt retreats and an invitation to join a "quilt-along," whatever that is.

And, from my own interviews, it seems the best way to get started is to find one such group. How? Find a local quilt shop and ask.

Crafts

Online definitions of what makes something a craft are lacking: "an activity that involves making something in a skillful way by using your hands, a job or activity that requires special skill."

I like what one of my craft-loving friends said better: "I am into fun arts, not fine arts," she said. "I have craft nights with girlfriends."

Fun arts. I like that. And judging from a plethora of online sites dedicated to the subject, so do a host of others. Crafters find fun in crafting. What are examples of these fun arts? My friend showed me a picture of restored furniture, Christmas decorations and clothes she and her nieces make for troll dolls.

And the online suggestions are legion.

Have a wedding coming up? Sellerstable.com says you can make bridal accessories like veils and purses, party favors, gifts for the bridal party and decorations like centerpieces and bouquets.

And you can sell your crafts. Fabulouslyfrugal.-com says the best selling crafts are personalized pet tags, bath bombs, bookmarks, keychains, magnets, jewelry, coasters, headbands, candles and lip balm. And each of these choices leads to others.

For instance, take jewelry. You can make necklaces, pendants, rings, bracelets, hair clips and earrings. Again, the choices are numerous. There is a website telling how to make earrings from ribbon, pearls, chain, thread or fringe, beads, wood, glass, wire, leather, feathers, bobby pins, lace, silver, old buttons or coins and rhinestones.

If you are reading this and would like to start crafting, maybe these suggestions will help. If you're a veteran crafter, you already have more ideas than the time to get to all of them.

Woodworking

According to Merriam-Webster.com, another definition of the word "craft" is "a skill in making things, especially with the hands," or "an occupation or trade requiring skill with the hands or as an art."

Thus, woodworking, defined as "the skill or art of making things from wood," is also a craft. And judging from my friends, I'd say it is a popular one in retirement.

What can woodworkers make?

Familyhandyman.com suggests over 40 outdoor projects, including benches, birdhouses, planters, picnic tables, wooden carts, garden arbors, decks and boardwalks. The same site suggests more than 30 indoor ideas, such as kitchen step stools, floating shelves, custom chess boards, shoe organizers, key hangers, storage cabinets and a desktop catapult (if you have grandchildren, I'd forgo the catapult).

Scrapbooking

Since we got married, Charlotte and I have gone from storing pictures in large boxes (where they were dumped with others regardless of time, date or theme) to plastic-encased albums, sometimes organized into trips or themes, to our smart phones, where the pictures are better quality but the organization is still bad.

No more. We've decided to join a movement called "scrapbooking," which, one online source says, dates back centuries to personal journals and diaries.

A scrapbook is a book that combines personal stories and reflections with corresponding pictures of the same. Physical books or folders can then add memorabilia (like a wedding invitation, newspaper clipping, obituary or wedding announcement.) I say "physical" because, today, scrapbooking can be completely digital, which makes it much easier (and you can still include pictures of the memorabilia).

Scrapbooking can be fun, as well as a great gift to future generations. So give it a try. A number of online programs can help, like Canva, Smilebox (creates shareable slideshows) and Artifact Uprising.

In addition, to make it easy, Storyworth.com lets you share online weekly stories with family, which are then collected and made into a nice keepsake book.

Home improvement

According to researchers at Harvard, Americans spent a record $420 million on home improvement projects in 2020. I'm sure many would point to the pandemic and subsequent shutdowns. Idle hands longed for something to do.

But I think it's more than that. Americans didn't only want something to do; they wanted something fun to do. And home improvement fit the requirement.

I'm guessing if we knew the age breakdown, retirees, even after 2020, make up a significant portion of home improvers, partly because it provides an opportunity for creativity. And, according to another Harvard researcher (Dr. George Valliant who studies longevity), "Creativity, like play, can turn an old person into a young person."

So if you want to feel younger and happier, here are my suggestions:

Inside your house

It's not exactly construction, but think about purchasing furniture (one piece or several). Part of the fun is the hunt, which means extensive research and shopping.

Consider restoring a piece of furniture, whether it's something you own or find in a resale shop or garage sale.

Could you both restore and repurpose something you find (maybe make a table out of an old door)?

Look for art work to create the right feel for a room.

Consider a major remodel (updated kitchens and bathrooms add value to a home).

Touch up your inside paint or go with a whole new color.

Towels, bed spreads and the like are inexpensive ways to add pizzazz to a room.

New flooring can give new life to a space (maybe a wood floor or new tile in the family room).

Consider replacement windows or, perhaps, a sunroom to let in more light. Studies show that more sunlight lifts your mood as well as your home's value.

Think about indoor plants, enough to enhance the beauty and enjoyment of your home, but not so many that they require too much work.

Think creatively about little things you can do. We had a craftsman build a pantry door out of beetle-kill pine (look it up). The piece made our kitchen pop.

In your yard

If you are lucky enough to have a yard, there are many opportunities to add attractiveness and fun to your life. Here are some:

If you like the beauty but not the work or cost, think about xeriscape (a desert look that requires little water or maintenance).

Nothing brings more beauty to your outdoor spaces than plenty of pots and window boxes full of beautiful flowers. Check with your garden center to find the right varieties for your area.

Consider an herb garden on your balcony or small courtyard.

Do you have unseemly cracks between cement or flagstone? Fill them with pretty ground cover.

Scatter wildflower seeds in rougher areas outside your yard.

Grow cherry tomatoes in baskets suspended from a fence or porch. There's nothing more tasty than fresh cherry tomatoes.

Go full on and plant a vegetable garden with tomatoes, cucumbers, sweet peppers, beans, carrots, squash, onions, peas and sweet corn. Consider raised planters for ease and beauty.

Grass softens things. Choose a variety and coverage you can easily maintain.

Rocks provide a nice highlight. Do an Internet search (it's part of the fun) to find just the look you want.

Stepping stones and pathways add interest and, sometimes, a hint of mystery or adventure. We have stairs made of railroad ties that ascend a hill.

Add benches and chairs for seating and the right look. I like brightly colored Adirondack chairs.

Umbrellas (maybe above outdoor tables) add both shade and color.

Consider a pergola above an outside sitting area. Will provide shade but allow plenty of sunlight, too.

Gazebos are both attractive and functional. One could hold a hot tub or be used as an outdoor kitchen.

Think about an outdoor kitchen or just get some outdoor appliances—cookers, smokers and such.

Water features add both beauty and enjoyable sound. Buy a self-contained one at a garden center or go big and create a mountain stream, waterfall and/or pond. Warning: ponds can add a lot of work.

Do you want to attract song birds? Make or buy bird houses (do your research and get the right fit for the birds you want). Also, think about color and shape—you want them attractive and functional.

Add bird feeders. Again, ask an expert about the birds you want to attract. Hummingbird feeders are popular. Position them to be seen from inside as well as outside the house.

Do you like the experience of a nighttime campfire? Construct a fire pit or buy a ready-made one. Think about benches or chairs for seating.

Consider adding a small greenhouse. You can grow your flowers here in the off season, and the structure itself will add a nice touch to your yard.

Think about fencing, especially if you need one for pets or small children. If possible, look around and find something unique. We have a small area outside our bedroom that is enclosed by a coyote fence (look it up).

Consider rock walls and metal or wood arbors where you can grow vines and highlight other features.

Plant trees that will thrive in your ecosystem and contribute to the look you want.

Consider outdoor lighting. With the new solar batteries, this is an inexpensive way to add intrigue and beauty to your landscape. We have solar lights along the stairs ascending our backyard hill.

11

Fun by the Dozens

F un Things to do at the Beach

- Wade in the shallows.
- Collect shells.
- Play soccer using a beach ball.
- Play beach volleyball.
- Build a sand castle.
- Build a sandman.
- Dig rivers and lakes in the sand.
- Draw or write messages in the sand.

- Get buried in the sand.
- Bury someone in the sand.
- Body surf.
- Lay out, grab a drink and good book and absorb the rays.

Fun Things to do in the Snow

- Make a snowman.
- Build a snow fort.
- Make a snow angel.
- Have a snow ball fight.
- Make snow ice cream.
- Ski.
- Snowboard.
- Go sledding.
- Go snowshoeing.
- Ride a snowmobile.
- Look for animal tacks.
- Go inside, sit by a fire and enjoy hot cocoa.

Fun on Halloween

- Decorate your house, inside and out.
- Make Halloween treats (caramel apples are good).
- Decorate cookies.

- Design or buy a Halloween costume for a child.

- Design or buy one for yourself.

- Go trick or treating.

- Entertain trick or treaters.

- Attend a Halloween festival.

- Visit a haunted house.

- Go on a hayride.

- Watch a scary movie.

- Sip a cup of pumpkin chai latte.

Thanksgiving fun

- Write a grateful list to get in the mood.

- Give an unasked-for gift to someone in need. Maybe do it anonymously.

- Volunteer to serve at a soup kitchen.

- Host a dinner. Invite family and others (maybe new immigrants).

- If family isn't an option, have a Friendsgiving. Might have to travel for this one.

- Have guests share something for which they are thankful.

- Say grace at the table.

- Cook something special (like turkey and dressing or pumpkin pie).

- Watch Macy's parade on TV.
- Watch football.
- Watch "A Charlie Brown Thanksgiving."
- Travel to see family.

Fun at Christmas

- Find and/or decorate a tree.
- Make and/or buy ornaments.
- Make and decorate Christmas cookies (try to distribute before you eat all of them).
- Create a snow globe (look online).
- Make a manger scene.
- Design and send personal Christmas cards.
- Browse a Christmas fair/store.
- Attend a Christmas program.
- Go to a Christmas Eve service at your church.
- If you have the chance, attend a Nutcracker performance.
- Share a gift opening with family or friends (helps if you include small children).
- Take a family photo.

Fun on the 4th

- Dress for the day (red, white and blue).
- Display Old Glory.

- Attend a parade.
- Be in a parade.
- Have a picnic afterwards.
- Grill hot dogs and burgers.
- Don't forget the dessert (nothing says the 4th like apple pie).
- Attend a baseball game.
- Enjoy a beach or lake (in a boat, if possible).
- Watch a fireworks display.
- Hold your own if you can (especially sparklers for the kids).
- Build a bonfire, and don't forget the s'mores.

Feel-Good Movies

- *Secretariat*
- *Groundhog Day*
- *It's a Wonderful Life*
- *The Shawshank Redemption*
- *Mr. Holland's Opus*
- *Hoosiers*
- *Return of the Titans*
- *Les Miserables*
- *Mary Poppins*
- *The Man from Snowy River*
- *Australia*

- *The Sound of Music*

Classic TV Shows to Make You Smile

- *Gilligan's Island*
- *Leave It to Beaver*
- *The Andy Griffith Show*
- *I Love Lucy*
- *The Dick Van Dyke Show*
- *The Flintstones*
- *The Waltons*
- *The Bill Cosby Show*
- *Little House on the Prairie*
- *The Brady Bunch*
- *The Beverly Hillbillies*
- *Green Acres*

Fun Must-See Zoo Animals for the Grands

- Red Panda—see at the Smithsonian's National Zoo.
- Elephant—Oklahoma City Zoo
- Bonobo—Milwaukee Zoo
- Giant Panda—Memphis Zoo
- Gorilla—the Bronx Zoo
- Polar Bear—Columbus Zoo

- Koala—San Diego Zoo
- Tiger—Cincinnati Zoo
- Lion—Henry Doorly Zoo in Omaha
- Giraffe—the Dallas Zoo
- Pygmy Marmoset—Lincoln Children's Zoo in Lincoln, NE
- Hippo—the San Antonio Zoo

Fun (and inspiring) True Stories

- *Endurance: Shackleton's Incredible Voyage*
- *Island of the Lost: Shipwrecked at the Edge of the World*
- *Alone on the Ice: The Greatest Survival Story in the History of Exploration*
- *The Long Walk: The True Story of a Trek to Freedom*
- *The Color of Water: A Black Man's Tribute to His White Mother*
- *The Glass Castle: A Memoir*
- *Seabiscuit: An American Legend*
- *The Forgotten 500: The Untold Story of the Men Who Risked All for the Greatest Rescue Mission of World War II*
- *Undaunted Courage: Meriwether Lewis, Thomas Jefferson, and the Opening of the American West*
- *The Boys in the Boat: Nine Americans and Their Epic Quest for Gold at the 1936 Berlin Olympics*

- *Unbroken: A World War II Story of Survival, Resilience, and Redemption*
- *Cry the Beloved Country* (a story of race and redemption in South Africa)

Favorite Retiree Hobbies

- Reading
- Traveling
- Walking/hiking
- Gardening
- Taking pictures
- Eating out
- Fishing
- Golfing
- Bicycling
- Bowling
- Learning a new language
- Playing a musical instrument

Hobbies You've Probably Not Tried

- Beetle fighting
- News bombing (showing up in someone else's filmed news event)
- Competitive duck herding
- Survival list prepping
- Cave diving

- Dumpster diving
- Bicycle polo (bicycles are used instead of horses)
- Ant keeping
- Knife throwing
- Mooing (yep, impersonating a cow)
- Collecting navel fluff (really?)
- Pole dancing. Seriously, it's on a list (mer-charts.com).

Your New Best Friend

Judging by how many retirees purchase one, it seems dogs really are man's and woman's best friend. Following are breeds that, according to the American Kennel Association, are popular choices. Choose one, and you just might be selecting your new best friend:

- Labradors
- French Bulldogs
- German Shepherds
- Golden Retrievers
- Poodles
- Beagles
- Pointers
- Dachshunds

- Welsh Corgis
- Australian Shepherds
- Yorkshire Terriers
- Siberian Huskies
- Shih Tzus
- Boston Terriers
- Pomeranians
- Cane Corsos
- English Springer Spaniels
- Shetland Sheepdogs
- Brittanys
- Cocker Spaniels
- Miniature American Shepherds
- Border Collies
- Chihuahuas
- Basset Hounds

12

Do It Together

Did you know that happiness is contagious? Well, according to a 20-year survey of 5,000 individuals, it is. A 2008 report by Harvard researchers found that "One person's happiness triggers a chain reaction that benefits not only their friends, but their friends' friends, and their friends' friends' friends. The effect lasts for up to one year."

I thought about it while putting the finishing touches on this book. Friends are necessary for happiness and fun, which can be a problem in retirement because many of us leave friends behind at the workplace. And if you decide to make a major geographical move, you separate from even more friends.

So this chapter is about finding new friends and maybe reconnecting with some old ones. Following are my suggestions:

If you're in a new city, you might join a service organization, a decision that seems to appeal to retirees. Thus, the average age for a Lion's Club member is 57. For a Rotarian, it's 58. Outside the U.S., the average is even higher, 71 for Rotary members in Australia, 74 in the UK. Reviews tell me that the meetings are fun and interesting in themselves, with the added benefit of supporting humanitarian efforts at home and abroad.

For something a little different, the Kiwanis Club motto is "Serving the children of the world," which is similar to Optimist Clubs where the emphasis is on building "hope and positive vision" in young people.

On a lighter side, the Red Hat Society is for adventurous women over 50, whom I have seen eating out in their red hats and purple dresses. Yep, I'd say they were having fun.

Do you enjoy speaking in public? Would you like to get better at it? Local Toastmasters Clubs include both the young and young-at-heart.

Do you like working in the soil and getting things to grow? Your local garden club will help sharpen your skill and introduce you to new friends who share your passion.

Are you an avid reader? Your local library or book store can help you find a good book club.

Are you fascinated with model trains and railroads? The National Model Railroad Association has clubs in most of the 50 states (Texas has seven by itself). Look them up online.

Do you like to bowl? I'm sure there are leagues to join at your local lanes.

Enjoy hiking and cycling? Others do, too. Search online for local groups.

Or consider hiking and cycling tours where the tour company supplies equipment, food, lodging and the new friends. For instance, Road Scholar offers trips along the Katy Trail in Missouri (America's longest Rails to Trails route), along the eastern shore of Virginia (might get a glimpse of the Chincoteague ponies) and a route from Vermont to Quebec and French Canada.

Also, Discovery Bike Tours promises "fine food and great lodging" on its tours around Crater Lake in Oregon, through the Texas Hill Country and along the coast of Maine.

If it's hiking you want, Road Scholar (road-scholar.org) has all-inclusive tours to places like Death Valley, a portion of the Appalachian Trail, the Canadian Rockies, Big Bend National Park in Texas and Acadia National Park in Maine. Also, there's Wildland Trekking, who offers a mule-assisted (they carry your stuff) three-day hike to the bottom of Grand Canyon and back (this one is on my list).

Are you a golfer? If so, you probably already have your buddies, but you can meet new ones, too. Check out the various scramble tournaments at your local course.

By the way, you can create your own tour. I've known golfing buddies to take multi-day trips to several nice courses (by van, or air if the locations are spread out). Similarly, some of my female acquaintances have girlfriend trips to see concerts or plays, to shop (maybe for antiques) or just enjoy a new place (a beach or wine country). Be creative. You could create a tour for old friends, grandchildren, cousins, school buddies—the options are limitless.

Are you in to restoring classic cars? So are others in your region. Search it online.

Did you know there are summer camps for adults? You'll find a list on Oprahdaily.com.

In addition, there are specialty camps for all ages, which, seems to me, might be a plus. Do some online searching. I've found camps for creative writers, harmonica players and bluegrass enthusiasts. I'm sure you can find one for your hobby.

And don't forget religious camps and retreats, which brings up another way to find new friends. I wonder how many of us meet them regularly at our place of worship. It will just take some initiative on your part to make the first move.

If all else fails, Meetup.com is an online service that connects people with the same interests. For instance, a hiking group will show events in your area that you can join.

And you don't need to concentrate on *new* friends. I agree with Dolly Parton and Kenny Rogers who sang, "You just can't make old friends" (check out their video on YouTube). Old friends already accept us for who we are. You don't have to "put on airs" with them, as my aunt used to say.

Old friends share memories that can be enjoyed all over again in the telling. And you can pick up where you left off with old friends.

So how do you reconnect? I'm sure you can figure it out for yourself, but I'll share my strategies:

Make a cold call, email or text. "Just checking in. How are you?"

If they live near you, meet for lunch (can include more than one, but no one unknown to the circle).

Go to your high school or college reunion. Plan ahead to get together with one or two of your closest friends.

Ditto for family reunions or work-related reunions. If you don't have one, organize it yourself (you can engage a few others to help).

If you live near old friends, create regular get-togethers (maybe a lunch with cousins or school mates every other month).

Some old friends plan yearly trips together. Maybe take motor homes or travel trailers and meet at a scenic place in the mountains or at a beach.

One more suggestion—retirees need intergenerational friends. I'm looking for opportunities to get with former students, as well as ways to engage grandkids one-on-one. Sounds like I may need to learn some video games.

13

What is Fun and Makes the World a Better Place, Too?

We have it on good authority that it is better to give than to receive (see Acts 20:35). And I'm pretty sure it's also more fun to give. It seems 25 million Americans think so. In 2017, they spent an average of 52 hours per year volunteering. So if you want to get in on the fun, here are some ideas:

Helping children

Volunteer to knit hats for infants in your local hospital, especially those in the NICU.

Go online to the Ronald McDonald House for sick children or the Make A Wish Foundation for terminally ill kids and see what you can do to help (they need money and services).

Put craft kits together for kids at St. Jude's Hospital. These might include coloring books, crayons and other items for a child in a waiting room. Check them out online.

In our area, you can give to Fill with Hope, an organization which distributes weekend snacks to underprivileged school-age children. They also need volunteers for packing and delivering.

Become a mentor with Big Brothers or Big Sisters, which will mean hanging out regularly with a child that needs an older adult (maybe grandparent) in his or her life.

Volunteer to help with your local Boy Scouts/Girl Scouts. They need both leader bees and worker bees.

Contact local elementary schools to see if they need folks to read to their classes. I'm pretty sure the answer will be "yes."

Reach out online to Samaritan's Purse and prepare a Christmas gift box for a child or children around the world (usually refugees).

Want to help your local children at Christmas? Contact your area Toys for Tots and go looking for a toy to drop off.

Become a CASA volunteer (an adult who acts as an advocate for abused children in a court of law). Search CASA online. They will train you.

Consider being a YMCA volunteer who can teach classes, coach athletic teams and mentor your area's youth.

In my locale, Kids Inc. needs coaches for kids' flag football, soccer, volleyball and basketball teams. Sound like too much running? Then volunteer for the T-Ball position.

Adults in need

Contact your local Food Bank or Food Pantry, who will take cash or canned food to give to the needy. Also, they can always use volunteers for packing and delivering.

Most cities have nonprofits who provide regular meals and lodging for the homeless. You can give money, cook or serve meals, and a host of other things. Contact your center for specifics. If you can't locate an agency, try contacting the Salvation Army.

Do you have wheels and a ready smile? Consider your local Meals on Wheels and distribute needed food to shut-ins.

Do you have construction skills? Your local Habitat for Humanity could use your help building new houses for deserving low income families.

Want to make a huge difference in the life of an uneducated adult (maybe a refugee)? Become an adult literacy volunteer. Teach someone to read and change a life in the process.

Have a heart for older people? Contact a nursing home about visiting with, reading to or maybe taking a walk with an older resident. There is a lot of room for creativity here. Could you teach a crafts class, exercise routine or lead a Bible study or song time?

Become a home hospice volunteer and do everything from visiting and reading, to getting groceries and cooking meals for your patient. This one requires a special kind of person, often someone who has himself or herself been through the dying process with a friend or family member.

If you like the challenge of an urgent and physically demanding assignment, talk with your local Red Cross about joining a Disaster Action Team.

Animals

Do you have a heart for pets? Your local SPCA needs volunteers to help with feeding and caring for dogs and cats.

Consider adopting a pet at your local pound. Those who do this claim it brings as much pleasure to them as it does the animal.

Want to rescue a dog but don't want a long term commitment? Consider fostering an animal. You keep the dog or cat until it can be adopted by an owner. And, yes, if you fall in love, you can adopt the pet yourself.

By the way, you can rescue/foster other animals, horses, for instance. Just look for a horse rescue center in your area.

Your faith/place of worship

I'm not going to offer suggestions here, but I'm sure much—maybe most—volunteering goes on because of one's faith. If that's the case with you, and you are not already involved, a phone call to local leaders or a conversation with likeminded believers will yield all the specifics you need to get started.

Random acts of kindness

You don't need an organization to practice volunteering. And you don't need specific programs to tell you what people need. Search the Internet and you'll find many ideas for serving others with random acts of kindness.

To supplement your research, I've come up with my own list. In doing so I had a guiding principle. These gifts had to come as a surprise, needed—but unasked for—by the recipient. So here are my suggestions:

Cook or buy some of the selections you liked in Bon Appétit (chapter 5) and take it to a single parent, sick person or shut-in.

Give one of the items you created in the Crafts section (chapter 10) to a family member, friend or complete stranger. Include a note telling why you made this item and why you want this person to have it.

Keep dining gift cards on hand to distribute to someone in need.

Pay a bill for someone who can't. You may need to do some sleuthing to identify the recipient. It helps to know church leaders, social workers, nurses, tow truck drivers and such.

Notice when someone's vehicle needs tires or repair and send an anonymous gift certificate in the mail.

Give slightly used clothes to someone in need. Better still, take him or her shopping.

Pay the restaurant bill for someone you don't know. First responders and military personnel are good prospects.

Mow the grass for or make repairs to the house of a shut-in.

Surprise a young, money-strapped couple with a night out.

Bake cookies for neighborhood children.

Give a special tip to a restaurant wait staff. This would be especially good at Christmas.

Write letters to soldiers (look online).

Help an immigrant family. Simply explaining the complexities of American life and culture will be greatly appreciated.

Likely, you have needy people in your own family. Surprise a child or grandchild with an unexpected gift (it doesn't have to be money).

Make your own list to add to this one.

Appendix

Hidden Travel Treasures

I've been asking retired people what hidden treasures are in their state, places I must see if I visit. Following are some of their recommendations. For some states, I've supplemented these suggestions with my own research.

Alabama

- Culman—Ave Maria Grotto is a rock garden that features 125 miniature reproductions of famous religious structures.

- Montgomery—The Hank Williams Museum houses the largest collection of Hank Williams memorabilia in the world, including the famed Cadillac where he tragically died at age 30.

- Montgomery—The Montgomery Civil Rights Memorial is dedicated to the "40 people who sacrificed their lives so the rest of the country could live in harmony."

- Alabama's Natural Bridge—This curved rock formation (148' long and 60'high) is the longest natural bridge east of the Rockies. It doesn't hurt that the picturesque setting of forest and natural gardens is simply beautiful. Add concessions and a gift shop, and it's definitely a place worth visiting.

Alaska

- Homer—a small city on Kachemak Bay on Alaska's Kenai Peninsula, known for its shops, art galleries, seafood restaurants and beaches.

- Kodiak Island—second largest island in the U.S., home to largest Coast Guard Base in the U.S. and the largest bears in the world (Kodiaks are larger than grizzles). Kodiak also is known for its superb fishing (salmon, halibut, rockfish, lingcod, rainbow trout and others).

- Wasilla—The Iditarod Museum is located in a log cabin and features trophies, photos and videos of dog sledding and its most famous race. There's also a gift shop and rides. Yes, rides. In the summer, visitors can take a cart ride pulled by real Alaskan sled dogs.

Arizona

- Antelope Canyon—slot canyons on Navajo land near Lechee

- Sedona—beautiful red buttes, lots of New Age shops, spas and art galleries

- Supai—village in bottom of Grand Canyon, not accessible by road

- Tombstone—home to the O.K. Corral where Wyatt Earp and his brothers shot it out with Clanton-McLaury gang

Arkansas

- Eureka Springs—called the "Little Switzerland of the Ozarks," quaint, extremely hilly, touristy town

- Hot Springs—spa town with naturally heated springs, located in the Quachita Mountains

- Jessyville—where you can dig for real crystals

- Murfreesboro—Dig for diamonds at Crater of Diamonds.

California

- Alcatraz—famous prison in San Francisco Bay, once housed Al Capone and Machine Gun Kelley

- Bolinas—known for its reclusive residents

- Fort Bragg—home to the Glass Beach, a shore full of colorful glass stone

- Los Olivos—small, historic town in Santa Barbara wine country
- Patrick's Point—now named Sue-Meg State Park, has dramatic beautiful coastline
- Tomales Bay—long, narrow inlet north of the Golden Gate Bridge, famous for oysters

Colorado

- Colorado National Monument—high desert land with sheer-walled canyons near Grand Junction
- Crested Butte—ski town with shops and restaurants located in wooden buildings
- Grand Lake—quaint town on the largest, natural lake in Colorado
- Grand Mesa—largest flat top mountain in the world, east of Grand Junction
- Ouray—called "America's Little Switzer-land," known for summer four-wheeling and winter ice climbing

Connecticut

- Essex—dubbed the "perfect, small American Town," art, shops and restaurants
- Gillette Castle State Park—looks like a me-dieval fortress. Take the tour.

Delaware

- Leipsic—Pick your own fresh, blue-craw crab to steam at Sambo's Tavern.

- Milto—Tour the Lavender Fields Farm where you can cut your own flowers.

Florida

- Coral Gables—Venetian Pool built in 1924, truly a unique public swimming pool

- Florida Caverns State Park—features a guided tour through a unique, limestone cave system

- Greenville Wacissa Springs County Park—an old-fashioned swimming hole

Georgia

- Cloudland Canyon State Park—Stairs into the canyon lead to a scenic falls.

- Cumberland Island—barrier island off the southeast coast, has feral horses

- Stone Mountain Park—best viewed from the Stone Mountain Scenic Railroad

- Tallulah Gorge State Park—spectacular 1,000' deep canyon with a falls

Hawaii

- Hawaii Volcanoes National Park—encompasses two of the world's most active volcanoes

- Papakolea "Green Sand" Beach—Yes, it has green sand and it's on the Big Island.
- Waimoku Falls on Maui—a strenuous hike but worth it

Idaho

- Twin Falls—Shoshoni Falls is higher than Niagra.
- Winchester—See Winchester Lake State Park, somewhat overlooked but good for catching rainbow trout.

Illinois

- Cave-in-Rock—Cave-in-Rock State Park has a one-mile, round-trip trail to the cave with nice views from there.
- Savanna—Mississippi Palisades State Park with great views of the river but no cell service

Indiana

- Brown County State Park—largest in the state, has hiking, biking and horseback riding
- Little Nashville—wineries and distilling companies, also music and theater

Iowa

- Burlington—See Snake Alley and Sterzings potato chips.

- Pikes Peak State Park—features a 500' bluff overlooking the Upper Mississippi River
- Winterset—known for its covered bridges
- Wolcott—Called "The Trucker's Disneyland," Iowa 80 is the World's Largest Truckstop.

Kansas

- Dodge City—Boot Hill Museum, Fort Dodge and more
- Liberal—The city hosts the Mid-America Air Museum and Dorothy's House (with photos and paraphernalia from the original Wizard of Oz). A Dorothy look-a-like will give you a tour.

Kentucky

- Lexington—Keeneland Race Track (go in April)
- Louisville—Kentucky Derby at Churchill Downs
- Mammoth Cave National Park (longest in U.S.)
- Slade—Red River Gorge, known for hiking and rock climbing

Louisiana

- Baton Rouge—Take the Great River Road along the back roads to New Orleans.

- St. Francisville—small, quiet town offers tours of five old plantations

Maine

- Bar Harbor—jumping off point for visiting Acadia National Park
- Baxter State Park—Located in the gorgeous north woods of the state, the park offers canoes and kayaks.
- Moosehead Lake—second largest lake in New England, exceptionally beautiful

Maryland

- Assateague State Park—Located on a barrier island, the park has camping, biking and horseback riding. The island is home to the wild Chincoteague ponies (which, by the way, don't live on Chincoteague Island but on Assateague).
- Solomons Island—Just off the coast of Baltimore, the island is unspoiled and uncrowded with shops, restaurants and museums.

Massachusetts

- Lexington Common or Battle Green—where the first shot of the American Revolutionary War was fired
- Nantucket—Wharves and cobblestoned streets are lined with restaurants, high-end boutiques and steepled churches.

Michigan

- Charlevoix—Earl Young mushroom houses were built in the early 1900s by this eccentric architect, and, yes, the structures, often referred to as "hobbit houses" or "gnome homes," do look like mushrooms.

- Mackinaw Island—located in Lake Huron between the upper and lower peninsulas. Go for the Lilac Festival in June.

- The Upper Peninsula—features quaint towns and wineries

Minnesota

- The Boundary Waters—one million acres accessible primarily by canoe, one of America's more remote and beautiful areas

- Duluth—Take the North Shore Scenic Drive from Canal Park north along the shore of Lake Superior.

- Ely—Wolf Center exists to "enhance the survival of the wolf internationally." By the way, Minnesota has the largest wolf population in the lower 48. And, yes, you can see live wolves at the Center.

Mississippi

- Windsor Ruins—Twenty-three standing Corinthian columns are all that is left of this cotton plantation built in 1861.

- Kiln—This small town has a big eatery, Dempsey's Steak and Seafood, where you can get amazing seafood and Cajun-inspired dishes along with sumptuous steaks.
- Natchez—St. Mary's Chapel is a beautiful Gothic church built in the 1800s as part of a plantation. Now it is hidden in woods and not on most tourist lists.

Missouri

- Table Rock Lake—Rent a pontoon boat at the Cape Fair Marina.
- Elephant Rocks Park—Take the self-guided trail to see these elephant-shaped boulders.
- Jacks Fork River—It's maybe the most scenic of all Missouri Ozark streams. See it from a canoe.
- Silver Dollar City—amusement park near Branson, has rides, dining and more

Montana

- Grasshopper Glacier—glacier in the Beartooth mountains, filled with frozen, extinct grasshoppers, only accessible July through September.
- The Yaak Valley—lush, remote and tranquil
- Allen's Manix Store in Augusta—This old-fashioned general store boasts "If we don't have it, you don't need it!"

Nebraska

- Lincoln—the National Museum of Roller Skating, home to the world's largest collection of roller skates

- Paxton—Ole's Big Game Steakhouse and Lounge has over 200 taxidermy mounts, plus a nice steak.

Nevada

- Eureka—The sign reads "Welcome to the friendliest town on the loneliest road in America." This charming little town on U.S 50 is 70 miles from other settlements.

- Goldfield—Santa Fe Saloon, the oldest continuously operating business in the state

- Las Vegas—The Burlesque Hall of Fame claims to be the world's only museum "dedicated to the history, preservation and future of burlesque." View hundreds of costumes and personal effects worn (*temporarily* of course) by the famous dancers. Yep, only in Vegas.

- Tonopah—Check out the Clown Motel and James the Bear at Tonopah Station Casino.

New Hampshire

- Gorham—For spectacular fall foliage, drive north to Berlin; then follow the signs for the Great North Woods Scenic Drive.

- The Monadnock region—Named for the mountain that dominates the landscape, the area is known for small and charming New England towns. Check out their seasonal activities.

- Mount Washington—Known for its extreme and erratic weather (in April of 1934, it recorded a wind gust of 231 mph), the mountain is the highest in New England. You can drive to the top, but only at regular hours and weather permitting so be sure to call ahead.

New Jersey

- Cape May—seaside resort known for its Victorian houses, shops and restaurants

- Hamilton—Grounds for Sculpture, a non-profit with intriguing art and sculpture exhibits inside and out

- Ocean Grove—resort town on the Atlantic, known for charming Victorian houses, restaurants and shopping

- Wildwoods Boardwalk—38 blocks of boardwalk with amusement rides, water parks, eateries, shopping and arcades

New Mexico

- Alamogordo—The New Mexico Museum of Space History is a world-class museum devoted to the history, science and technology of space travel.

- Chimayo—El Santuario de Chimayo is a Roman Catholic church and national historic landmark famous for the story of its founding and as a contemporary pilgrimage site.

- Glen Rio—Russell's Truck and Travel Center has a free antique car museum, containing a spectacular assembly of muscle cars from the '50s and '60s.

- Hatch—Known as "the Chile Capital of the World," Hatch puts on an annual Labor Day festival that draws thousands of chile lovers from across the nation.

New York

- Corning—Corning Museum of Glass is "dedicated to the art, history and science of glass" and has amazing displays.

- Finger Lakes Region—group of 11 long, narrow lakes, beautiful, natural scenery, interesting small towns and state parks, wineries, breweries and distilleries

North Carolina

- Asheboro—The North Carolina Zoo is the world's largest natural habitat zoo.

- Boone—Located in North Carolina's Blue Ridge Mountains, Boone is the entryway to

Daniel Boone Park and the Hickory Ridge Living History Museum.

- The Outer Banks—barrier islands off the coast, pristine beaches, state parks and water activities

North Dakota

- Medora—small town with big history. Tour the Chateau de Mores and visit the national park.

- Theodore Roosevelt National Park—Take the scenic loop drive to view the badlands where Teddy Roosevelt once lived. You'll see lots of bison, elk and prairie dogs along the way.

Ohio

- Hocking Hills—Ohio's "scenic wonderland" is home to nine state parks and state forests.

- Mansfield—famous for the prison where *Shawshank Redemption* was filmed, for auto racing and for the Richland Carrousel Park in downtown Mansfield

- Put-in-Bay—You'll need to take the ferry to visit this island on Lake Erie. Attractions include live entertainment, an historical museum and beautiful water views.

Oklahoma

- Commerce—home of Mickey Mantle and site of a Bonny and Clyde shoot-out

- Medicine Park—Founded as Oklahoma's first resort town, you'll not find anything like it in the state.

- Oklahoma City—Oklahoma City National Memorial and Museum honors the victims, survivors and rescuers from the bombing of the Alfred P. Murrah Building on April 19, 1995.

- Tulsa—original house and movie set for The Outsiders with Patrick Swayze, Diane Lane, Rob Lowe and Tom Cruise

Oregon

- Astoria—The city boasts many history sites, including The Lewis and Clark National and State Historical Parks, the Astoria Column with murals depicting area history and the Columbia River Maritime Museum, which showcases fishing, shipping and military history (appropriately housed in a water-front building).

- Crater Lake—the deepest and maybe prettiest lake in the U.S. See the write-up in "Intended for Pleasure" (chapter 3).

- Multnomah Falls—Two million visitors a year think this the most beautiful spot in the Pacific Northwest.

- Willamette Valley—With more than 700 wineries, the leading wine region in Oregon is famous for its Pinot noir.

Pennsylvania

- Gettysburg—Known for the battle that marked a turn in the American Civil War, the town is replete with history. The Gettysburg National Military Park contains the Gettysburg National Battlefield Site, the Gettysburg Museum and Visitor Center and the Gettysburg National Cemetery (where a memorial marks the site of Lincoln's 1863 Gettysburg Address).

- Grand Canyon of Pennsylvania (Pine Creek Gorge)—The 45-mile-long gorge is nearly 1,500' deep and offers hiking and biking on the Pine Creek Rail Trail.

- Kutztown—small town of Dutch ancestors known for the Mennonite carriages that plod along its roads and for an annual Folk Festival, which claims to be the oldest continuously operated folklife festival in America

- Lancaster—One of the oldest inland towns in the U.S., Lancaster is known for its large Amish population and its relaxed way of life. Visitors enjoy the rolling hills and well-kept farmland as well as the plentiful antique stores.

Rhode Island

- Newport—where you can take a tour of the harbor in the 72' Schooner *Madeleine* (for land lubbers like me, it has SAILS) or take in some history at Fort Adams State Park

- Ocean Drive—Also in Newport, Ocean Drive passes by a number of points of interest, including King Park, the New York Yacht Club, Fort Adams State Park, a U.S. Coast Guard Station and Brenton Point State Park.

- Narragansett—Known to the locals as "Gansett," the town was the summer vacation spot for America's rich and famous during the gilded age. Be sure to visit the Towers, which was the gateway to Narragansett Pier Casino, a high-stakes gambling establishment no longer standing.

- New Shoreham or Block Island (the first is the town, the second, the land it sits on) is the smallest town in the smallest state in America. You'll ride the Point Judith Ferry to get there where you can enjoy 10 square miles of restaurants and shops.

South Carolina

- Beaufort—Tour pre-Civil War mansions on Port Royal Island.

- Boykin— Mill Pond Steakhouse is just the spot for a top of the line steak in a remote, historic setting.

- Conway—Luvan's Fish Camp Restaurant serves generous portions of fresh seafood.

- Hilton Head—Dresden Beach is a hidden treasure on Hilton Head Island.

South Dakota

- Deadwood—Old West town where the likes of Wild Bill Hickok and Calamity Jane lived, now home to tourists and casinos

- Hot Springs—Black Hills Wild Horse Sanctuary. The name says it all.

- Keystone—With a winding road, scenic bridges and tunnels, Iron Mountain Road is an alternative route to Mount Rushmore and Custer State Park.

- The Lakes at Custer State Park—There are five, all drop-dead beautiful with swimming, canoeing, paddle boarding and nearby food and lodging.

- Sturgis—home to the annual motorcycle rally that draws thousands of leather-clad enthusiasts. Eat at Uncle Louie's Diner.

Tennessee

- Crossville—The Minister's Tree House is a giant tree house built by a preacher who said God told him how it was to look.

- Lynchburg—Jack Daniel's Distillery was established in 1866 by one Jasper Newton Daniel. Tours daily.

- McMinnville—Cumberland Caverns provides several levels of tours (easy, moderate and extreme) and is host to live concerts.

- Pigeon Forge—The Titanic Museum is shaped like the RMS Titanic and pays tribute to the ill-fated ship, passengers and crew.

Texas

- Canyon—Panhandle Plains Historical Museum is the largest of its kind in the state. Explore artifacts of the Old West and stroll through a replica, late 1800s West Texas town. Then head out to Palo Duro State Park, 12 miles to the east and the second biggest canyon in the nation.

- Fort Davis—The University of Texas McDonald Observatory, 15 miles northeast of town, conducts daily tours of their incredible, modern telescopes and photos of space. You'll also want to visit the small town of Fort Davis, the highest town in Texas and home to one of the best preserved Army frontier forts in the southwest. In addition, Fort Davis is important as home to the 24th and 25th U.S. Infantry and 9th and 10th U.S. Cavalry, all of them exclusively African American units established after the Civil War.

- Fort Worth—The Stockyards National Historic District once saw millions of cattle shipped to markets in the north. Now the area abounds in western-themed restaurants and shops. Don't miss the daily longhorn cattle drive through the city streets.

- Fredericksburg—A town founded by German immigrants in the beautiful Hill Country of Central Texas, Fredericksburg is known for its wineries and authentic German cuisine.

- Marfa—This small, desert town in West Texas is known for its arts center and mysterious "Marfa Ghost Lights" that sometimes appear in the night sky east of town.

Utah

- Capitol Reef National Park—Take the less-traveled dirt road to Temples of the Sun and the Moon, formations that look like sails and seem to appear from nowhere.

- Dead Horse Point State Park—The view has been compared with seeing the Grand

Canyon from the south rim; plus it's not crowded. See it at sunset.

- Goosenecks State Park—The overlook looks down on the mighty Colorado before it plunges into the Grand Canyon.

- Needles Overlook in Canyonlands National Park—See my comment on Dead Horse Point.

- Peek-a-boo and Spooky Canyon are slot canyons deep within Grand Staircase-Escalante National Monument. This is a tough hike so come prepared.

Vermont

- Burlington—Lone Rock Point on Lake Champlain is a favorite with kayakers.

- Dorset—Emerald Lake, with its rich colors of water and pristine lakeside beaches, plays host to a variety of kayakers, paddle boaters, canoe enthusiasts and swimmers.

- Ripton—Robert Frost Trail. Like all of Vermont, it is gorgeous, but I'll go there to pay homage to my favorite poet.

- Rutland—Wilson Castle. Constructed in 1867 by a Vermont physician who wanted to impress his English wife, the stately red building has turrets and towers, which rise from massive walls. The interior is just as impressive. You'll want to take the tour.

- Smugglers' Notch State Park—The winding road, known as Smugglers' Notch, is a narrow pass that cuts through the Green Mountains. In the early 1800s it was used by smugglers trying to circumvent U.S. trade restrictions with Canada. Today, Smugglers' Notch brings tourists to a state park and ski resort.

- Waterbury—Beginning in Waterbury, the Green Mountain Byway runs for 71 miles through some of Vermont's most scenic country. Enjoy open meadows, fertile farmland and lush forests, all with a stunning mountain backdrop.

Virginia

- Cape Charles—This small city with Victorian-era houses is located on a peninsula near the mouth of Chesapeake Bay. Stroll through the historic district, bird watch at Kiptopeke State Park and top it off with a seafood feast at Shanty Restaurant.

- Duffield—Natural Tunnel State Park is a 300-yard natural tunnel (big enough to support a railroad line) running through an Appalachian mountain. Tradition says that

Daniel Boone was the first Anglo to lay eyes on it.

- Gordonsville—Described as a "charming southern town of quaint shops and galleries," Gordonsville is located 19 miles northeast of Charlottesville. Visit their Civil War Museum, located in an old hotel which once provided care for 70,000 soldiers, both Confederate and Union.

- Occoquan—This quaint town in Prince William County is a suburb to DC. Tour the Mill Museum, picnic at River Mill Park and check out the one-of-a-kind shops along Mill Street.

Washington

- Mount St. Helens—Having last erupted in May of 1980, killing 57 people, Mount St. Helens is still an active volcano. You will want to view the before and after pictures at the Visitors Center.

- Hurricane Ridge—The most easily accessed mountain area in Olympic National Park, the ridge is snow-covered for much of the winter but is still open year-round.

- San Juan Islands—You will need to take a ferry or passenger ship to view these stunning islands off the northern coast of Washington.

- Seattle—Pike Place Market is the most famous shop on Seattle's wharf. It's known for the unique delivery system of fish to customer. Employees wrap the slimy catch-of-the-day and toss it to the outstretched hands of eager buyers.

- Snoqualmie Falls—In a state of exceptional waterfalls, this one is the most visited and it's worth every bit of the 1.4 mile, out-and-back hike.

- Walla Walla wine country—With over 120 wineries, the region is recognized as one of the best wine countries in the nation.

West Virginia

- Blackwater Falls State Park—At the heart of the park is Blackwater Falls, a 62' cascade where the river enters rugged Blackwater Canyon. This Allegheny Mountain treasure is known for scenic bike rides and boating.

- Harpers Ferry—Harpers Ferry National Park, which includes the town of Harpers Ferry, commemorates John Brown's raid in 1859 that, some say, began the Civil War. Despite its painful past, the area is known for its imposing beauty.

- Monongahela National Forest—With over 900,000 acres of forest land, the park attracts over three million visitors a year. Enjoy hiking,

biking, horseback riding and boating while looking at some of West Virginia's highest mountain
peaks.

Wisconsin

* The Apostle Islands National Lakeshore—
  The Apostle Islands are a group of 22 islands
  in Lake Superior off the northern Wisconsin
  coast. The area boasts nine lighthouses, more
  than seen in any other national park. You'll
  have to get to these beauties in a boat, your
  own or aboard the Apostle Islands Cruise
  Line.

* Fish Creek—Peninsula State Park is called
  Wisconsin's "most complete state park,"
  with multiple campsites, a summer theater
  and 18-hole golf course.

* La Crosse—Grandad Bluff is a 600' bluff
  overlooking the city. Less than four miles
  from La Crosse, the drive takes about 12
  minutes. Locals recommend going at night.

* St. Croix Falls—St. Croix National Scenic
  Riverway is a canoe enthusiast's paradise.
  With 250 miles of protected rivers in Wisconsin and Minnesota, you can enjoy a one- or
  multi-day trip.

* Spring Green—House on the Rock is the cre-
  ation of Alex Jordan, who, in the 1940s, saw
  a chimney rock and imagined what it would

be like to build a house on it. The massive structure contains architecturally distinct rooms, streets, gardens and shops. The grounds include a 27-hole championship golf course. Visitors can choose to either stay or tour this one-of-a-kind resort.

Wyoming

- Aladdin—Aladdin General Store is a throw-back to an earlier time when one mercantile establishment had it all. In operation for more than 100 years, its inventory includes knickknacks and antiques.

- Cody—The Buffalo Bill Center of the West has five museums. Browse artifacts from the American West, learn about the famous fron-tiersman's life through a multimedia display and walk through a recreated frontier town with log cabins and a museum.

- Hartville—Miners and Stockman's Steak-house is housed in the state's first bar estab-lished in 1862. But the atmosphere is not the only selling point. Sit down and feast on one of the state's best steaks.

- Sheridan—The Trail End State Historic Site was once the Kendrick mansion, built in 1891 by cattleman John B. Kendrick. For a small fee, you can take a self-guided tour of this massive house and grounds.

Acknowledgements

Several people have made this book possible. Once again, Rob Henslin worked his magic with the cover design. Rich Bullock did his usual, excellent job with the inside pages. And professional artist Lee Baughman provided the whimsical chapter illustrations (his forte is water color. Take a look at www.facebook.com/lee.baughman.10).

In addition, the following people served as content specialists, advising me in specific subjects like art, crafts, travel and food: Lee Baughman, Claudie Biggers, Nancy Brent, Melinda Fletcher, Mike Haynes, Lynae Jacobs, Melisa Munch-Soegaard and Glenda Moore (Glenda works with kindhousebakery.org where proceeds go to feed the hungry in Ukraine).

Carolyn Crow provided copy editing, an especially hard task with so much technical detail.

And friends and family kept me motivated. Thanks, especially, to Shug Bonds, Steve Beckham and, as always, the lovely Ms. Charlotte.

About the Author

As a popular newspaper columnist, award-winning college professor and bestselling author, Mike Bellah has been writing to and about the baby boom generation for over 30 years.

His first retirement book, *The Best Is Yet To Be: Discovering the Secret to a Creative, Happy Retirement*, challenges conventional wisdom by suggesting that more money is not the greatest need of retirees. "What if there's something else, something that costs nothing, but something that will supply all you need (including the funds) for what could be the happiest years of your life?"

Dr. Bellah's second work on the subject, *The Best Retirement Gifts Are Free*, tells readers how they can retire successfully, even in a pandemic.

Now, on a lighter note, Bellah's latest release is *1001 Fun Things To Do in Retirement*. Fact filled, fast paced and witty, the book is a practical guide for adventuresome boomers.

Married for over 50 years, Mike and Charlotte Bellah have five children and 10 grandchildren. They live in the retirement home they built in a little Texas canyon where Mike enjoys biking, hiking and working at his retirement gigs.

Also by Mike Bellah

The Best Is Yet To Be: Discovering the Secret to a Creative, Happy Retirement

When college professor Mike Bellah took an early buyout, he expected the golden years to live up to the carefree, happy times pictured in magazine ads. But, within weeks, the reality of lost identity and limited funds left him panicked and depressed. In this book, Dr. Bellah uses extensive research, personal narrative and real-time blogs to explain how he got his hope back, and, with it, discovered the secret to a happy retirement.

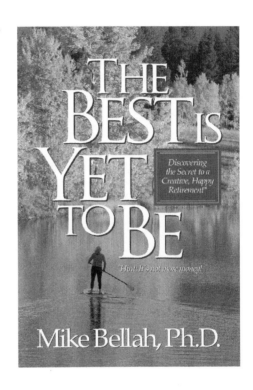

The Best Is Yet To Be Journal: Write Your Way to a
Creative, Happy Retirement

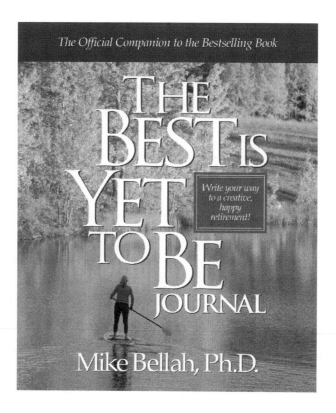

According to Bellah, "The most important story you will read on retirement is not mine; neither is it one written by any other author. The most important story you will read is your story, the one you will write, the one that will shape you as you shape it, the one that will help make your dreams come true."

The Best Retirement Gifts are Free: How Do You Retire in a Pandemic?

• How do you retire in a pandemic?
• What are the best retirement gifts?
• Can you make up for lost time?

In his 2nd book on retirement, Dr. Bellah interviews friends, reviews books and movies, chases a two-year old, dines with a middle schooler, hangs out with brothers, celebrates a wedding anniversary, takes walks and bike rides, and gives readers what they've come to expect from him:

Honest and hopeful answers to the questions they are asking.

Written with dozens of brief vignettes, *The Best Retirement Gifts Are Free* is an ideal gift book.

The Fun Side of Retirement - Podcast

Tired of being lectured about social security, Medicare and the financial parts of retirement? Ready to hear about the fun side? In this popular podcast, Mike Bellah teams with childhood friend Eugene "Shug" Bonds to talk about retirement, nostalgia and good, old-fashioned fun.

The program was paused in July 2021, but you still can enjoy 26 laughter-filled episodes. It's free. Just search for "fun side" on Audible, Amazon, Buzzsprout, Apple, Spotify or other podcast platforms.

Made in the USA
Columbia, SC
20 June 2022

62000820R00109